W9-DIL-121

The Strategic ATTITUDE

Integrating Strategic Planning into Daily University Worklife

Nathan Dickmeyer

NACUBO

Library of Congress Cataloging-in-Publication Data
Dickmeyer, Nathan.
   The strategic attitude : integrating strategic planning into daily university worklife/ by Nathan Dickmeyer.
      p.cm.
Includes bibliographical references.
ISBN 1-56972-027-4
1. Universities and colleges—Business management. 2. Strategic planning. I. Title

LB2341.92.D53 2004
378.1'06—dc22

                                                          2003071038

National Association of College and University Business Officers
Washington, DC
www.nacubo.org

Printed in the United States of America

ISBN 1-56972-027-4

CONTENTS

Chapter One
INTRODUCTION

> In olden times strategy was listed among the
> Ten Abilities and Seven Arts as a beneficial practice.
> It was certainly an art but as a beneficial practice it was
> not limited to sword-fencing. The true value of sword-fencing
> cannot be seen within the confines of sword-fencing technique.
>
> Miyamoto Musashi, *A Book of Five Rings*

A college or university* administrator immersed in strategic thought searches out the decision option that best moves the institution toward its vision. Like "sword-fencing," the true value of strategic thinking is invisible if we look only at its technical results: missions, plans, and projects. The art of strategy is immensely complex and requires strategic thinking to approach today's challenges.

Strategic planning at many universities these days focuses on honing the mission and developing projects with measurable goals. Unfortunately, the preoccupation with these technical pieces of strategic thinking often leaves daily operations unassisted by what could be gained from consistent reflection on the many other requirements of strategic thought. Daily operations need a context. Team members need to be able to evaluate why one project or option might be more important than another. Mission and projects get all the attention, but other key elements of strategic thought, including fully articulated strategies, values, principles, and concepts require daily attention to have a positive effect on operations. Strategic planning should not be an independent project. Daily decisions must emanate from strategic approaches. The values and strategies of the institution must be well known and accepted for decisionmaking to have a context.

The inspiration for this book comes from over 200 campus experiences as a consultant, chief financial officer, member of accreditation teams, and higher education researcher and writer. In visit after visit I found institutions engaged in a planning process or just finishing a planning process and unable to describe the benefits of the process. I saw universities unaware of the principles they needed to live by, justifying decisions and projects with little reference to a coherent strategy and surprised by problems that had been creeping up for years. One recent visit

---

*I use the words university, institution, and college interchangeably. These ideas apply to any higher education institution.

was unusually thought provoking. The university had been engaged in a strategic planning process for three years. It had developed an elaborate system for communicating and reassessing the plan each year. The process had led to a reinvigoration of the mission statement (well, one word was changed, but it was an important word) and had resulted in a rather long list of important projects on which to focus institutional resources. I could not find, nor did I hear, what success looked like (vision), what they had to do to achieve success (strategies), or anything about the distinctive ways they would pursue their success that would make them proud (values stated in principles). There was no real rationale for the projects, nothing that justified or prioritized the projects. The projects just seemed to be "a few of my favorite things."

This book is intended as a guide to daily work life in a strategic organization—an organization that operates with an effective understanding of its environment, in the direction of its mission, and within the constraints of its values. The goal is to move planning from a project to a part of daily work life. To achieve this goal, strategic thought must be broken into its many components and we must see how each aspect of strategic thought can be incorporated into an approach to decisions that helps move the institution forward.

The Strategic Attitude builds on the work of George Keller in *Academic Strategies* (1983). Keller initiated a call for universities to be more responsive to their environments and avoid the static creation of a blueprint by planners. This book looks at the world proposed by Keller and asks, "What is the CFO's role in it?" This book explores strategic thinking from the chief financial officer's point of view.

Robert G. Cope, in *Opportunity from Strength: Strategic Planning Clarified with Case Examples* (1987), built on Keller's work and added case studies of organizations changing to confront their environment. This book takes the lower road, examining what needs to be done from day to day to make an organization strategic. Rather than case studies, this book uses fictional vignettes, "days in the life," of CFOs and others on campus to demonstrate the problems of the classical approach to planning and to show more effective strategic thinking "on the job."

Daniel James Rowley and Herbert Sherman, in *From Strategy to Change* (2001), add an excellent analysis of strategic choice within each of the higher education segments. They present many examples of major strategic choices made within the last decade, both successes and failures. The work that follows will give CFOs an orientation on how to foster successful strategic choice through daily work and decisions for the next decade.

Michael Finnerty (1992) discusses the role of the CFO in planning at Yale University. He describes much of the role as "reactive." The limitations appear to result from Yale's definition of strategic planning to include only academic planning. Since Yale apparently perceived little need for strategic alterations, it required only financial support for altering its curriculum. This book is intended for those institutions that are finding their world in constant and challenging flux—a world that demands a strategic approach to change.

This book will begin with an analysis of common practices in planning and managing, tying each element, whether success or failure, to the strategic-thought framework. Then it will explore in greater depth the neglected areas of strategic thought—conceptual thinking, strategic thinking, principles, and learning through reflection, auditing, and assessment. Finally, the book will explore how administrators, especially chief financial officers, can best manage within this framework. It will look for shortcuts and daily exercises that establish the condition for strategic management, strategic leadership, and institutional learning.

Good strategic development requires that many types of minds come together to think in different ways. This book has been written to appeal to thinkers of many styles, each with his or her own ways of learning. Deductive readers will enjoy the lists at the chapter ends that encapsulate the key ideas of the preceding chapter. Other readers will find the extensive amplified enumerations within the chapters to be of greatest help. Finally, the more inductive readers will find the stories at the ends of the chapters to be the most persuasive, hinting at problems, giving living examples of work, and developing the threads from which we learn during our daily lives.

The intended effect is to save universities the hundreds of thousands of person hours now spent on planning, while improving university management by imbuing daily work with a strategic orientation.

Chapter Two

ADOPTING A
STRATEGIC ATTITUDE

What exactly is a strategic attitude? *Strategic thought* is a description for the system of organized thought that must be adopted to perform work with a strategic attitude. Successful engagement in the thought process produces a *strategic attitude*. The attitude produces a guide for action.

The phrase *strategic thinking* rather than *strategic planning* is used throughout this book, because the implication of planning is of a project to be done outside of day-to-day work. Thinking is something we do constantly. And a successful strategic orientation requires us to think about our goals every day.

The two- to three-year planning project needs to be replaced with daily activities and a different orientation to daily decisions. This book lays out the activities, building on pieces of strategic planning projects that have brought success and adding many more. The daily activities include:

1. Delegating environmental scanning
2. Clarifying university values
3. Asking, "What is the strategic thing to do here?"
4. Rewarding strategic behavior
5. Questioning the strategy
6. Evaluating the strategy, the mission, and the principles
7. Ensuring organizational learning
8. Playing a leadership role in affirming strategies, mission, values, and vision

THE STRUCTURE OF STRATEGIC THOUGHT

Figure 1 shows the simplest system within strategic thought, which here is called the *main line*. Traveling down from beliefs to action, we are going from highly abstract to more concrete levels. We begin with beliefs. Beliefs are those ideas we hold, fairly universally, about higher education, including the purposes of universities, our ability to improve the lives of people, and the importance of the creation of knowledge.

FIGURE 1
Structure of Strategic
Thinking—Main Line

BELIEFS
Learning
Knowledge
Personal Transformation

VISION
The Future
Goals

STRATEGIES
Academic
Marketing
Financial
Service

ACTION
Decisions
Leadership
Communication

The main basis for our formation of a vision for the institution rests on our beliefs. Our beliefs shape our vision of a "perfect" future for our university. The vision becomes the goal set. Several other influences on vision are shown in later figures.

Strategies are the broad directions we will follow to achieve our vision. Our ideas of direction are often within our own spheres of influence, for example, academic, recruitment (marketing), finance, and service strategies. These strategies need to be firm enough to guide behavior. Some people call very-detailed strategies tactics. To avoid drawing a distinction, I prefer calling these just lower-level strategies. This book spells out ways of developing strategies and using them.

Strategies are only necessary if our vision requires change. If all we need to do is become more efficient in the way we do things or change other people's image of us, then we only need to carry out our current ways of doing things better. This does not require strategic thinking. Strategies are only needed if the organization, in response to a changing environment or a new vision, must alter itself fundamentally.

We then must use strategies to guide our actions. Our actions are tangible decisions and intangible things like leadership and communication. This book promotes the understanding of the structure of daily work life well enough to see how planning can benefit from strategic influences.

In figure 2 we add two new ideas: mission and concepts. Mission is shown as derived from beliefs and influencing the vision. We cannot decide where we want to go until we know who we are. We define universities by the audiences they serve and the ways they serve them.

Concepts are those ideas and systems we must learn in order to develop effective strategies and put them into action. As new strategies are tested and new modes of action are examined, new concepts must be learned. Hence, the arrows between concepts and strategies and between concepts and action point in both directions.

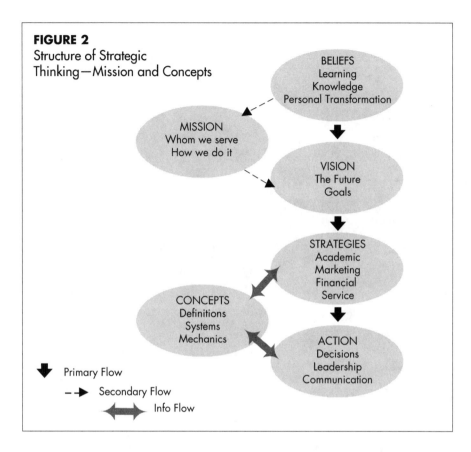

FIGURE 2
Structure of Strategic
Thinking—Mission and Concepts

As concepts become more sophisticated, strategies and actions are influenced and as strategy or action moves to new levels, concepts must be revisited.

Figure 3 adds two more ideas: values and principles. Specifically, the values are those that make our university distinctive and define how we go about doing things. They are also an influence on the vision, but we take our stand with them when we add them to our principles.

Principles are the statements we make to communicate how our vision is to be met with strategies within our values.

Figure 4 adds the feedback loops. We audit our work, looking to see if the goals in our vision are met, or at least approached. In this manner we review our strategies. Were they effective?

We also think deeply about the more abstract ideas. We think about our beliefs. Now that we have made progress, have we learned some things that might make our beliefs more sophisticated? We also reexamine our values, and as our values are clarified, our principles must be restated.

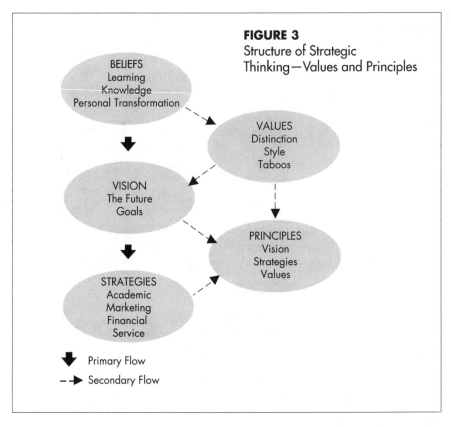

FIGURE 3
Structure of Strategic
Thinking—Values and Principles

Figure 5 puts all the subsystems on one page. The main line is simple: we go from beliefs to action. To get to the vision, however, we rely on an understanding of our mission and values. Principles help us tie values and vision to strategies. All around are the cycles: concepts mutually influencing strategies and action, while auditing, assessment, and reflection require us to review our more abstract ideas based on the results of our actions. Organizational learning occurs when we can remember our concepts and reflections.

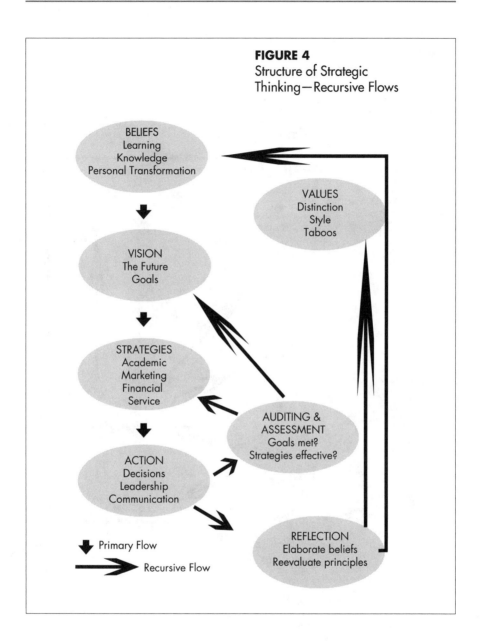

FIGURE 4
Structure of Strategic
Thinking—Recursive Flows

BELIEFS
Learning
Knowledge
Personal Transformation

VALUES
Distinction
Style
Taboos

VISION
The Future
Goals

STRATEGIES
Academic
Marketing
Financial
Service

AUDITING &
ASSESSMENT
Goals met?
Strategies effective?

ACTION
Decisions
Leadership
Communication

REFLECTION
Elaborate beliefs
Reevaluate principles

Primary Flow

Recursive Flow

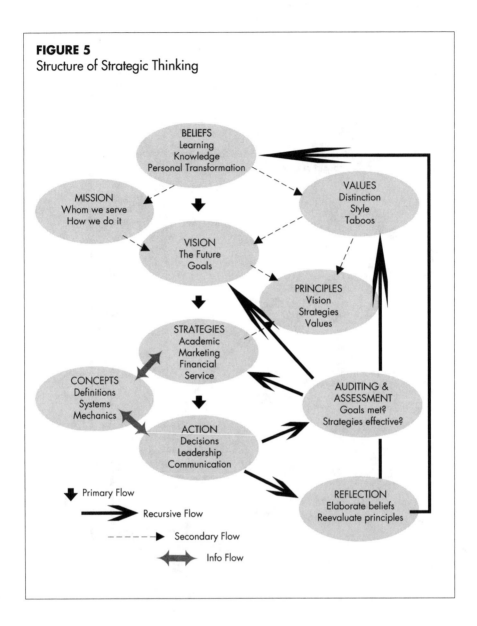

FIGURE 5
Structure of Strategic Thinking

Seven Key Thoughts

1. What's important in guiding day-to-day challenges is not a plan or a
    list of priorities, but a flexible, strategic attitude about the future and
    the direction in which the university must go. Without a strategic at-
    titude, the day-to-day business of work can lead anywhere.
2. If strategic planning exercises leave administrators' future orienta-
    tions, and hence day-to-day decisionmaking, unchanged, they prob-
    ably are a waste of time.
3. A strategic attitude in the university setting is the willful search for
    ways to provide the most desirable learning experiences for the group
    of people the institution has chosen to serve. The view of the future
    when that is achieved is called the vision. The pursuit of that vision
    is enhanced by a series of small choices, made by all members of the
    organization, that reflect an understanding of the best-known strate-
    gies to move the organization toward the vision.
4. A strategic attitude gives people a framework within which all
    members of an organization choose among their various workday
    options.
5. The strength of agreement within an organization on a strategic
    vision and the appropriate strategic attitude will correlate with orga-
    nizational success.
6. Strategic attitude can be visualized as the mental effort of picking up
    an organization and pointing it in a new direction, through the sea of
    competitors and other challenges.
7. A strategic plan that makes no mention of how to look for new
    opportunities—in technology, in partnerships, in new learning inter-
    ests—will not be useful today. Most planning exercises result in crude
    roadmaps through the suburbs, but the future is a wilderness, and
    success comes not with a street map but with a guiding star. Five years
    ago would we have predicted the current, shaky finances of the states,
    the rise of for-profit education, the faltering job market for graduates,
    and the growing reluctance of givers?

Chapter Three

THE GULF BETWEEN PLANNING AND OPERATING

Most strategic planning processes are not integrated well with day-to-day management flow. University chief financial officers face the constant challenges of negotiating competing demands, acting as a buffer between the university and external pressures, handling emergencies and people problems, and setting priorities and designing systems and procedures for future needs. But when it comes to planning for strategic change that would rationalize and streamline these functions and would move the university in new directions, most universities fall back on time-consuming, multiyear exercises that celebrate what the university has done and revalidate an often-contradictory wish list of projects that never get started. Planning as it is currently done under these circumstances takes away from our ability to operate, rather than enhances our competitive fitness.

THE DAY-TO-DAY WORK OF THE CFO

As we currently understand it, especially those of us who are CFOs, operating is our job. We make and announce decisions, we work with others and influence decisions, and we communicate our ideas to others. We differentiate administrators from staff members by the level of discretion they have. In this sense, staff members "do" and administrators "choose." Nevertheless, almost all staff members have some level of discretion. Even those entering numbers into the computer can choose whether to think of a better way to accomplish the task. Likewise, the opposite also holds true: administrators also enter numbers into the computer. The real work of CFOs and other administrators comes in many forms.

Negotiating for common ground. It seems like negotiating never ends with others inside and outside of the campus community. Other administrators often ask us: "Who does what?" Then we negotiate. Students often begin their negotiations with a version of, "Do I really have to follow this policy?" Staff members confront the CFO with, "Can you stop her from doing that?" We look for the end point. We decide what we absolutely cannot give on. We search for common ground. Given competing interests, we must make choices. (See March and Simon [1958, 156] for an analysis of situations that lead to bargaining as opposed to rational choice.)

Serving as a buffer. A primary CFO function is to buffer the organization from environmental shocks. CFOs develop contingencies, limit the risk of investments, hire security guards, and make reports to regulating agencies. In each of these cases, CFOs must develop options and make choices on what buffers to employ and in what manner.

Handling emergencies. Why must the CFO be consulted when there is a burst steam pipe, when someone forgets to order check stock, when the bookstore vendor gives the required 90-day notice to end its contract, when the students take over a building, and when a faculty member is badly cut throwing away an old monitor? There are good reasons, because the CFO is good at making emergency decisions and because there are always financial implications. There are also not-so-good reasons, as when the CFO has power and one would not want to do something he or she did not approve of or because the CFO seems to be the only one who makes decisions. Nevertheless, for all those events not covered by standard operating procedures or policies, someone who will take responsibility for not having the time to "consult widely" must make a choice. The more "policy free" the institution is, the more ordinary events have to be treated like emergencies. The choice of how best to react must be made quickly.

Solving people problems. Can you imagine the day when the behaviors of your colleagues are completely predictable? The human being is not the only animal that understands he is hurt, but humans have taken that understanding to a very high level. The job of an administrator, it sometimes seems, is to manage pain. Everybody hurts. This one doesn't get the respect he thinks he deserves. The habits of one person are an insult to another. One person's cultural imperatives are another's annoyance. Selecting appropriate ways of recognizing and easing pain is central to a manager's work.

Setting priorities. This is one aspect of leadership that most distinguishes the excellent from the mediocre. Giving focus to the efforts of others is a difficult task. People just roll through the day until someone says, "This is important. The other things are necessary, perhaps even critical, but this one thing is important to me. Do you understand what that means to you? Do you have any ideas on how we can get it done, by tomorrow?" Choosing what is really, and I mean *really* important is critical to leadership.

Designing systems and procedures. Administrators do this more than others, but they do not have to own this aspect of work solely. Redesigning systems requires a good understanding of whole systems—all the minute interactions with other systems. It also requires comprehending just what a good system does.

While administrators have a broader view and a stronger sense of the purposes of systems than staff members do, staff members very often understand the importance of interactions with other systems best. For me, this interactive piece of work life has always demanded much attention. Designing complex systems often involves hundreds of choices.

Working on exceptions. Yes, this is the famous 10 percent of everything that takes 90 percent of our time. If any regular set of interactions with students involves 100 factors—major, courses taken, start dates, level, ethnicity, age, grade point, academic progress, ability to pay, and so forth—and if there is only a 1 percent exception rate, then it is likely every student is an exception. (One percent of 100 is 1.) What about the graduate student who must take an undergraduate course and who wants to pay the undergraduate rate? What refund do you give to a student who drops out just one week after starting and the student's start date, allowed only with copious petitions, was three weeks after the last date to add classes? What about the staff member who teaches a course but who wants her adjunct pay to go to her administrative department? Ever have a student attempt to pay with a gold bar? Choices, choices, choices.

I've left out the project side of operating, including bringing up new student and financial systems or moving an office to wireless communications. The theme of this list is choice—not just administrator choices, but also choices made by all members of the organization. Although the flavors of the situations change mightily, they all seem to involve choice. There are times when one must just sit there and take it, but these times are few and can hardly be fitted with the name, "work."

THE IMPORTANCE OF PLANNING

Strategic planning for many, many universities is a once-every-five-years-big-deal project. These days we make "living documents" so that the exercise can be continued forever. Our plans don't sit up on the shelf gathering dust. We take them down once a year, dust them off, and report to the trustees on our progress. Of course, this does get a little embarrassing when we have to report that progress on *priority number one* has been minimal. Nevertheless, we can talk about the new plans that we have for *the plan*. That said, a number of good outcomes can result from planning exercises.

Mission. Planning processes often begin with a deep look at the mission statement (Rowley and Sherman, 2001, 195–96). Although the most frequent result is a simple rewording, the process is remarkably beneficial (Pearson, 1999, 163). Institutions remind themselves of their historical importance and their successes

(Tracy, 2003, 36). They rededicate themselves to serving the groups well that they were founded to serve (Dunn, et al., 1992, 33).

In a few cases institutions are able to use the experience to realize that they are doing much more than the original mission and doing it well. The creation of a new mission that captures that broadened service dedication is a difficult, but ultimately fulfilling, pursuit. The exercise becomes a celebration of what the university has become.

One institution took years to understand that its mission bore little relation to its actual strength. As a women's college, it saw itself as an "eighth sister." That is, it was dedicated to women's education, rather expensive, and striving to attract academically elite women "of the best circles," but falling short. Its mission dedicated it to these ideals. A talk with the director of placement, however, revealed the truth—a beautiful truth, not an ugly one. (The depth of understanding of student transformations found in placement offices always justifies a visit to that office.) The people in placement saw the entire student body transform from timid but bright women of uncertainty to self-assured women of business. In fact, the purpose of the college was not to attract elite, polished young women, but rather to imbue students with those qualities over their years at the institution. The true advantage of the college was the network of successful alumna who supported a brilliant summer internship program. Many strategies, from financial aid to recruiting, hinged on the exploration and ratification of the new, explicit mission.

Not all mission-renewal exercises end in success. As one example, a committee of representatives from 23 academic departments at one university came to the conclusion that the mission of the college was to explore knowledge in just 23 academic areas. Some institutions fail to realize that missions are not just slogans. Slogans are "of the times" and serve the narrow purpose of drawing a broad range of possible clients closer. In many institutions, however, the start of strategic planning offers a chance to carefully examine the mission.

Vision. Planning exercises often result in useful vision statements. Vision statements differ from mission in that they give more than a purpose; they inform the university community about what success will look like for them in the future. Kouzes and Posner (2002, 125) call it "focusing on the ideal" and write that these statements can give organizational members a "sense of meaning and purpose. . . ." Often presidents develop the best statements. Sometimes planning committees or planning vice presidents come up with robust, visionary statements, but presidents are most directly responsible for thinking about how they would like to mold the institution. Presidents are given license to say things like, "I see a university where our feeder high schools are strengthened by partnerships with our academic departments and where we facilitate the support and volunteer efforts in these schools by private business."

A good vision statement is written interactively with the development of strategies and values. A strategy to develop partnerships between the university and school districts, bringing in private businesses, suggests a future state for a vision. If the vision comes first, the strategy is suggested (Dunn, et al., 1992, 28–29). Mission and vision statements are among the more successful products of current planning exercises, because they are at a level of abstraction that is comfortable for university executives and because agreement is easier to build with abstract ideas than with concrete plans. Most presidents fare better with global ideas on the future of the institution than with operational ideas on pricing policy and financial aid formulas. Committees find it easier to agree at the level of belief, mission, vision, and principle than on the best actions to carry out. In fact, most committee work breaks down in disagreements about how the committee should operate—the most concrete level. It is also difficult to keep discussion at the abstract level. Committee members want to toss in their favorite solutions to all the university's ills at the earliest possible moment. I still remember the lengthy Cold War debates over table shape. We can agree that nuclear weapons are bad, but please don't ask us what color the napkins should be at lunch.

Nevertheless, good committee leadership waits until all the solutions are in the ring, then sweeps them up, puts them aside, and pushes the focus to the discussion of vision. This requires mastery of the flip chart. Sheets are labeled "Solutions," and as they are filled up, they are ripped off and posted in a corner. Every time a committee member drifts back to his or her favorite university-saving solution, the leader must say, "Yes, here it is. We haven't forgotten it. Now, what else might the ideal future look like?"

Projects. Speaking of solutions, current strategic processes are magnificent in the lists they produce of projects. These are the great ideas that are terribly important. Most of them are copies of good ideas undertaken by peer institutions. Many are necessary to catch up with the competition or "best practices" gleaned from books, surveys, or observations of other universities or even companies. The projects lists are often long. In most cases measures that would indicate successful implementation are annotated on these lists. At many institutions, after publishing the lists with the mission and vision (the "Strategic Plan"), trustees begin expecting annual updates. They want to see priorities and timelines. They want reports on the measures. Because these projects are quite concrete, disagreement is very possible on the relative worth of the ideas. Unfortunately, institutions avoid disagreement by including nearly all of the suggestions on the lists. The decision of what *not* to do is never made. In practice, many projects languish for lack of funds, management time, and interest. There seems to be a wide gap between what would be required to fulfill everything on the lists and the budget. Few projects have brave promoters who arrive with grappling hooks and ropes and swing across the abyss.

Those projects that are pushed to action and bring about change in the institution almost always lead to improved practices and competitive position. Rowley and Sherman (2001, 17) urge universities not to leave competitive advantage to businesses. Certainly, the energy added to moving the ideas forward by the planning process is very helpful. In this way, current planning processes have assisted many institutions. Nevertheless, all too often the projects represent improvements only to the life of the promoter and seldom benefit the institution as a whole.

Too often the list of projects lacks any strategic framework. How does the institution as a whole change? Is this change such that the institution is more likely to reach its goals? Does this come from any sort of grand plan, or does each represent someone's "little plan"? Without a framework it is very difficult to say what must be done first. We do what is easiest. We do the president's favorites. We do the ones with the most vociferous proponents.

You and everyone in your organization must know why you all are doing what you do every day on the job. One of the most difficult parts of planning and the most important piece that needs to be integrated into everyday thinking is at the middle levels of strategic thought. As noted above, every organization has a terrific set of "end results," projects that must be accomplished "according to the plan." In fact, however, these "planning projects" may be the same one or two projects each member has carried around for the last five years as solutions to the problems facing the organization. Ever walk in on a committee that already has a dozen solutions? Ever try to find the problems these solutions are solving? Ever try to figure out what the rationale could possibly be for some of these "solutions"? What intellectual framework exists that would allow us to figure out why one solution might be better than another?

The middle ground that takes us from the mission to what we are doing is a bloody minefield. The mission is too vague to tell us why we should do what we must, to give context to the way we manage, what we choose to do first, how we must decide, and what we must do to live up to our values. The middle ground includes the strategies, principles, values, and concepts we must understand to judge whether what we are doing is moving the institution toward fulfilling its mission. Because the mission describes an interface between the institution and its environment, strategies are needed to guide alignment (Rowley and Sherman, 2001, 22).

The excellence that we seek in developing strategies runs into roadblocks because such a level of development requires superb knowledge of the environment:

the needs and perceptions of the people we wish to serve, the organizations that seek to fulfill the same needs we intend to fulfill, and the wishes and needs of our supporters. Our block with developing values is that we don't like to talk about the obvious. Of course we want to help others; of course we want to avoid causing harm to anyone; of course we are a family; of course we want our employees to look forward to work . . . but what values make us special and differentiate us in a way to help make us successful (Dunn, et al., 1992, 31)? Finally, concepts are just plain hard. Explain to me again why I'm only getting $45,000 a year out of a million-dollar endowment. Why is it that asynchronous online instruction may achieve more learning than a series of lectures? Why is intellectual property important to me?

Closing the gap between strategies and daily work requires a continuous appraisal of the environment, a strongly affirmed strategic direction and decision processes that are guided by that strategic direction. A small college may note that its career-oriented graduates falter in the current economy. A community college may note that public support of both operating and capital needs is waning. A state comprehensive university may observe that senior-level students have begun piling up as students move increasingly slowly toward graduation. Stage one requires a deep understanding of these trends and their causes. Do liberal arts graduates of the small college have trouble finding first jobs, but after five years progress to positions of greater responsibility than career major graduates? Are space and financial resource limitations forcing the community college to limit the ways it can serve its community? Are financial pressures causing upper level students at the state institution to take more and more demanding jobs, slowing their progress to degrees?

The daily work of designing budget systems, designing information systems, setting customer service policies and procedures, determining the fit of job candidates, and choosing the next project to undertake can then be guided by a new strategy. The new strategy might be limiting majors to the liberal arts and including career-oriented instruction to the requirements of special certificates for the small college moving toward training for success all through life. For the community college it might mean moving more offerings to asynchronous learning over the Internet to reduce demands on facilities. For the state institution pricing might be shifted through differential tuition or financial aid to reduce net tuition cost as the student nears degree-receipt.

As later chapters will show, however, grand strategies alone are not sufficient. An institution must know what success looks like, be certain of its values, understand the workings of its systems and environment, be willing to state its direction as principles, and be strong enough to evaluate its failures and successes.

A Day in the Life: Joseph d'Ordinaire, CFO, Beltway Community College

At 6:00 a.m. Joe woke to "Lite FM" and stretched out his hand to silence Elton John. He quietly left his bed, hoping not to disturb his wife. While shaving, he remembered he would probably be late again tonight and would miss his daughter's soccer game—another planning meeting. The key themes committee met every Tuesday at 4:00 p.m., and last Tuesday he was with them until after 7:00 p.m. They had been working on the theme, "the pursuit of excellence," and had gotten bogged down in attempts to define "excellence." He remembered the old adage that the more inconsequential the battle on campus, the more heated the tempers.

His role on the committee was important. He often mediated disputes between the "Excellence Clique" and the "Access Commune." He also tried to remind people of the possible financial effect of their ideas. Because of his effectiveness in these roles, he was well respected in the campus community. Nevertheless, he was unable to sustain this discipline and was chagrined every time someone found it shocking, occasionally even insulting, that his or her idea had to stand a financial test.

Later that morning in his office, he began to put together a recommendation for next year's revenue estimate. He had heard rumors from the state education office that tuition was not going up next year. He also had the enrollment forecast from the admissions office. "Pretty optimistic, as usual," he thought. County support looked grim: he knew that there would be no increase, and he hoped that there would be no cuts. He wondered if he should propose some symbolic cuts to protect the core of the budget. He thought maybe he could propose to save $250,000 in county money by doing away with the development department. Every year he tried; every year he failed.

The state revenue formula was unlikely to change, if tuition was kept level. This meant that almost everything rested on enrollment. His old strategy of making his own enrollment forecast and keeping the probable shortfall budgeted in a contingency had worked up until this year, when the president had found the contingency and "reallocated it." Now he was scrambling with hiring freezes and spending cuts because even his forecast had been a little optimistic.

Later in the afternoon, he was still putting numbers into the spreadsheet. Good numbers spelled heavy cuts to any proposed budget; fiction spelled trouble by October. He ran his fingers through his thinning brown hair. While working on the numbers, he had negotiated a new lease on the storefront campus in the Crystal Place Shopping Center and had lumbered through two one-hour employee reviews. He had known that there was no getting out of the lease, despite the disappointing demand at the site. He found the reviews tiring and repetitious as he paced through the forms provided by Human Resources. He had also authorized a large wire transfer and had asked the assistant controller to stop working on the bank reconciliation and fill in for one of three absent cashiers.

He had Bob, his assistant, bring him a bowl of soup from the cafeteria for lunch. The donuts and bagels the staff brought in had kept him going so far, not to mention the coffee. Still, with an hour to go before the "Excellence Wars," he couldn't shake the feeling that something was missing.

What *was* a good revenue projection? How could he make sense of the process? He had great spreadsheets, but he could not find a direction to go. What could justify the lease? What was he supposed to tell his employees about the future when they asked during the employee reviews? What did the future hold? He had mouthed the words about "customer satisfaction" and "commitment to excellence," but frankly, he didn't have a clue what they really meant to him. Of course the bank reconciliation had to balance. Of course revenues had to go up and accounts receivable down. He and his staff were excellent about that and always had been. He also believed he had turned the corner on customer satisfaction when he fired Darcie Gray. It had taken him three years, but finally the union couldn't find a hole in his case. She had been just awful with students, faculty members, and the others in the office.

Finally, he searched in his mind through the key themes that had been proposed so far for something to hang on to. "Excellence for the Community," "Access for Action," "Barrier-free Education," "Diversity for Success," and "Preparation for a Lifetime" rang out to him. The key themes seemed to hold no "keys" for solving the problem of his revenue estimate.

Just then James Fister, a professor of English, stuck his head in the door. "Joe," he said, "Do you have a minute to talk about the meeting this afternoon? I'm really worried that the 'Forces of Darkness' are forgetting what we at BCC really stand for." The professor chuckled and sat down.

Seven Key Thoughts

1. Too often the lists of projects, which supposedly come out of planning, existed long before the exercise began—there is no value added.

2. The range of daily demands on a university CFO, or any administrator for that matter, requires mental agility and a strong ability to make decisions. If planning is to be meaningful in an organization, it must have an effect on the day-to-day decisionmaking, the "here and now" of an organization.

3. Current planning practices have only a modest effect on the "here and now." Cookbook planning exercises allow many discoveries, but the results are often too rigid to be useful in an ever-changing world.

4. The gulf between planning and operating exists because planning doesn't speak and operating doesn't listen. Critical questions must frame the plan; for example:
    a. If budgets are to be affected, what would a plan look like?
    b. If tuition, scholarships, and other pricing decisions are to be influenced, what should a plan tell us?
    c. Does the strategic plan tell us how risky a capital budget can be?

5. Good strategic planning processes ask the hard questions:
    a. Whom do we really serve?
    b. Whom could we serve?
    c. What should we stop doing?
    d. How do we find opportunities?
    e. What is changing around us that should change us?
    f. What are we not very good at?

6. Successful strategic plans answer these three critical questions: 1. What will we look like in five years if we are successful (the definition of success)? 2. What are the three most important things we must do to succeed? 3. What are the three most important obstacles we must overcome before we can proceed in our quest for success?

7. Finally, a good strategic plan begins with an answer to the basic question: Why do we exist? What can we do to satisfy the needs of a population, or several populations, in a way that keeps us competitively, environmentally, and financially responsible and successful? What makes us special? The middle ground must be filled with real strategies, strong principles, difficult concepts, and felt values.

Chapter Four
THE CONTEXT FOR DECISIONS

Infusing day-to-day institutional work with an attitude of future success requires that we more deeply explore the concept of day-to-day work. A stronger understanding of decisionmaking on the basis of two major premises can guide us toward ways of relating planning to our daily operational needs. The first premise is that choices and decisions are the aspects of work that strategic attitude and thought should influence, if any organizational change in the desired direction is to be accomplished. The second is that decisions are social events, often requiring the interaction of large numbers of people over time (Cohen and March, 1974, 85).

CHOICE

Many aspects of day-to-day work change the course of the university, that is, influence the image, competitiveness, size, efficiency, effectiveness, and social relations of the university. These are the events that foster, for example, a change in the quality or scope of academic programs, a change in tuition price, a change in target enrollments, a change in support, or a change in staff or student satisfaction—that change its "fitness for competition." These are the events that change its success in obtaining resources. All these events of interest involve either choice or environmental change. We decide a tuition change. Our competitors set their tuition. Notice, however, that choice is a component of both types of event. We choose to raise tuition. We also may choose to stay under a competitor's tuition increase, or we may choose to ignore the information. We can also choose not to even look for the information on competitor pricing. Even changes in the environment present choices.

There are many, many events that do not involve choice, and there are choices that are not terribly interesting. The publicist who puts the new tuition in a brochure is not choosing the new price. The choice has been made. He or she is implementing it. Implementation itself, however, is full of choices. Should the tuition price be in bold 16 point or italic 6 point? Black or gray letters? To the CFO, these may not be interesting choices, but choices they are.

A mark of today's service organizations, especially universities, is the amount of choice making that goes on at all levels. The manufacturing establishments, perfected by Henry Ford, all strove to drive choice from the workplace. Service organizations have brought choice back. This has happened largely because the interface is not between man and machine; it is between man and man.

The complexity of the interface between two people does not allow the degree of specification that was possible when the relationship was between man and machine. We simply cannot predict all the questions, challenges, ideas, theories, and sentiments that one person can present to another. As a result, even our lowest-level customer support person in the bursar's or registrar's offices cannot be given a script that works in all situations. Almost all staff members must exercise discretion.

Compared with Henry Ford's original production lines—one color, one model, one line speed, one motion—today's universities are workplaces of constant choice. Many of the smaller colleges I have visited have had more majors at various degree levels than faculty members. The combinations of loads, scholarships, grants, loans, and work have produced almost as many separate net prices as students. Instructional modalities now include classrooms, laboratories, seminars, independent studies, videotapes, asynchronous computer instruction, studios, semesters abroad, broadcast videos, narrowcast video, credit for experience, internships, research, capstone courses, and credit for hands-on work. Each of these can have pricing and billing implications. Do you want to work in an office 9 to 5 or telecommute? Teach in the classroom or teach from home with distance learning? Courses meet from 7 a.m. Monday to 11 p.m. Sunday, unless you like the 2 a.m. on your computer shift.

Students may be 18 and just out of high school. They may also be 55 and working full time, or just off of welfare with three children and two grandchildren. Students are eagle scouts and felons. Students can be master's degree candidates, staff members, Ph.D. applicants, and community volunteers all at the same time.

There is no formula that gets a black model-T off the line every 38 seconds for us. That's why our days are filled with constant choice. No situation seems exactly like the last. No appeal to the market works every time. No rule of thumb works well every time.

In the university environment, we make daily choices at the policy level (for tuition and aid formulas) and at the individual level (for exceptions and the style of communication with the students). Do we call the need-based scholarship a "Nathan University Grant" or a "Presidential Excellence Scholarship"? Do we mail the student a jumble of federal rules and specifications listing the various awards, or do we call the student with congratulations and walk her or him through the next steps? Do we send the award letter to "Dear Student," "Dear Mr. Dickmeyer," or "Dear Nate"? When we call home, are we prepared to speak only in English, or are we ready to speak in English, Spanish, or Vietnamese? These are the choices we make each day.

Chapter 11 of this book concerns integrating daily decisions into strategies. In that chapter we will examine how to move from the reactive mode of, for example, raising tuition to cover a budget gap to the strategic mode of viewing the tuition decision within the context of strategies to, for example, better assist students toward timely degree completion with targeted scholarships to junior- and senior-level students. The first step in moving into the strategic mode is to become more aware of decisions as the core of day-to-day work and to evaluate them more in terms of strategic directions.

THE SOCIAL CONTEXT OF DECISIONMAKING

While we stereotype decisionmaking as a president sitting at his (not her—this is a stereotype, right?) desk, saying, "Yes," or "No," the truth about choice is considerably more complex. Decisions are, in fact, long social processes, where the final direction is a result of influence, interaction, presumptions, predilections, and predictions about the reactions of others (Dunn, et al., 1992, 42).

By "social" I mean that decisions are arrived at in an organization in a variety of ways, all of them a result of both the real reactions of people to available options and the presumed reactions of other people. Also, both people and organizations make decisions. That is, the president can say, "Tuition will increase by 6.5 percent"—a person makes the decision. Conversely, the whole organization can be involved. The idea of an increase somewhere between 5 and 8 percent can be part of a two-month discussion that ends with most people presuming that it will be 6.5 percent. With the former, an individual can be said to make the decision (influenced, of course, by the presumed and known reactions of others). With the latter, no individual appears to be the actual decision maker, but the process of putting the budget together brings about a level of comfort (or inevitability) about the tuition increase.

As one example, the State University of New York (SUNY) recently planned a tuition increase of 46 percent after years without an increase. The tentative announcement seems to beg reaction. The years when students took over buildings in reaction to talk of tuition increases has ended. The decision will be final only when the law is passed and the state education department writes the regulations. Yet, the whole process is caught up in "Albany politics." The governor is confronting the legislative leaders with his constraints. Lobbyists from the campuses, including professionals, faculty unions, and loose student collectives are all descending on those they think they can influence. The budget was due three months to the day before I wrote this passage. I have seen New York State budgets (and final instructions on the tuition price) come out in mid-September—after the affected school term has begun. This decision is far from one man "deciding" in his office. A better metaphor would be "social upheaval," even war.

The social structure of a decision is determined by the culture, especially those elements of culture that determine the distribution of power. Some organizational cultures have a tribal decision-making style. Other organizations have the patience and need for unanimity of a meeting of the Society of Friends. Nothing is decided until all hearts are one. And still other organizations have enshrined the democratic ideal. "We will discuss this for 20 minutes, then we will vote. The majority wins." This culture replaced the central authority model in the Western world and is used more for community governance than organizational governance. The model has carried over into universities and remains a strong cultural component of academic governance (Cohen and March, 1974, 116). Since most choices are among many options, each of which advantages subgroups to differing degrees, choice often requires coalitions, compromise, and creativity.

Cultures can create decision-making styles that pull from many models, simultaneously and sequentially. Presidential cabinets can thrash through an issue like warring princes before the queen or king, then switch to passionate pleas to bring their fellows to their side, like a Society of Friends. In desperation, they may appeal to democratic ideals and take a vote. In the end, the president may ignore the majority and take a completely different tack, like a sultan. Like good tribesmen, the warring princes lay down their lances and try to figure how to bring the rest of university into the fold with the president's decision.

More decisions are made in the style of the SUNY tuition decision than in the style of a formal decision made by one person or committee. Salaries with bargaining units or quasi-bargaining units are often negotiated with positions and ideas floated between parties. Trade-offs are added, using benefits to allow one side to gain more without as much loss to the other side.

The "budget decision" is an enormous social project. In many campuses the level of participation is quite high. The budget-request document advances goals and rationales and lists assumptions. It also gives guidelines for making and justifying a request. These guidelines are rarely followed exactly, but the results are all useful for gauging the intensity of feeling about alternatives, support, and risk. Yes, we, the administration, could just present them with their budget, but we need to get commitment to the budget, we need new ideas, and we need to bring their expectations in line with reality. What the president and CFO give up to get commitment, new ideas, and lowered expectations is a degree of discretion. Others get to influence the outcome. In some cases their influence is substantial. The path to a "final budget decision" winds through many people in the organization. The budget is socially constructed reality (using a phrase from Berger and Luckmann, 1966).

The picture painted here is one that shows how individual choices, often in the form of the smallest influence, can change the direction of the university. These choices are arrived at by individuals influenced by others or by whole organizations reacting to ideas. Chapter 12 of this book discusses leadership in a strategic organization. Decisions move organizations forward on a day-to-day basis, but the decision process, as we have just seen, is often complex. For that reason, imbuing an organization with strategic intent requires a leadership team that provides a compelling vision and clear strategic directions for getting there.

THEORIES ABOUT DECISIONS

The more knowledgeable one is about decisions and the way they change organizations, the easier it is to use strategic thinking to influence the direction of change in an organization.

Decision-making power gravitates to those willing to make them. There seems to be some sort of positive-feedback loop working in these situations. When a person makes a decision, and things go reasonably well, the person may feel better about themselves, and others will increase their confidence in him or her. As the person's confidence grows, more and more people bring decisions to him or her. Others may have a negative experience with making a decision. In fact, one negative experience may be sufficient for a person to start avoiding making decisions. Because the negative cycle always leads to an abrupt end, there often are only a few people eager to make decisions. The young who have not yet had bad experiences are willing, but there are far fewer willing people who have had the experience of making decisions. The exceptions are those with some immunity. Presidents seem to have more immunity. There are fewer people in the organization above them who can sanction the decisions they make. Still, in organizations the willing are greatly outnumbered by the unwilling: the decision avoiders.

As a result supplicants come to the willing bearing decisions from far lands to be made. These issues seeking decision are often not technically a part of the purview of those willing to make decisions. Nevertheless, the organization would run better if the decision were made. Several models can be used to handle these situations. The decider can attempt to empower the "bearer." "That's very interesting. What would you do? Well, that sounds like a very good direction. While I can't say that you must do that, I certainly support what you wish to do. Take it to Charlie and say that I like the idea."

You can also involve the sovereign more directly. "Wait a second. . . . I'll call Charlie now and tell him I like the idea I hear coming out of his office. That should make it okay." Finally, you can give the decision your imprint and take responsibility for it. There are many decisions that have ambiguous authority ranges. You can stake your claim. The CFO can say, "To simplify the billing process, all independent study courses must be for 12 or fewer credits. This is actually an academic decision, but it works as a finance decision."

Decision avoiding is deciding. This is a common concept. If you do not choose an option, you are generally choosing the status quo. In a forced-choice situation or where the status quo has no answers, you are choosing uncertainty and, often, that someone else will make the choice, as above.

Decision avoidance is more than turning away a subordinate who has a question. It is also not probing a plan or an idea to search for possible future choice situations. It is a pathological reticence to face a choice situation. Many people avoid unpleasant choices. It is extremely unpleasant to choose what must come out of a budget when funding drops. It is really not pathological to try to avoid pain. Nevertheless, the result of avoidance is usually greater pain. Some people, however, evade even simple choices. Remembering the shame of a mistaken choice is enough to cause him or her to avoid any search for choice. The shame, like the pain, arrives unbidden anyway. The choice then is a surprise, and because of its new gravity, it must be carried "up the line" for a weightier determination. More immunity is needed to make an emergency choice, now presenting itself without benefit of research or prethought.

Decision avoidance is anathema to strategic thought. Strategic thought requires anticipation and preparation.

All decisions are gut decisions. No matter how much we learn of a situation, no matter how carefully we have studied historical outcomes, no matter how carefully we have surveyed opinion to gauge reaction, we choose with our heart (or stomach to keep the metaphor with the same body part). Because we cannot predict the future very accurately, even with really good information, we still must use the "fuzzy" part of our brain to fill in the blanks. March and Simon (1958, 136–71) built the original case that man has only limited resources for handling complexity. Our goal should be to inform our "gut" as well as possible and reduce the size of the blanks, but we can never erase them. That is why we have to use data to inform our more complex nature. Our cogitating design for "fuzzy" thought is incredibly advanced and not at all captured in the circuitry of our rationally designed computers. We can use the hard numbers, the probabilities based on history and trends, and the stochastic model results to inform, but we cannot let them make the decision (Emery, 1979, 232).

Decisions before their time are denied maximum information. Making a decision before the last possible minute robs the decisionmakers of the latest information. This last possible moment includes time to prepare everyone for the consequences—"communication" we call it. Learning the preferences of others only after making a decision can be devastating. If the decision was made at the last possible moment, however, the devastation should be shrugged off. If the decision was made, announced, and implemented (10,000 brochures printed) early, and then new information came in, devastation is warranted. When an organization is faced with a decision, always ask, "When is the last possible moment for making this decision? Why?"

Ratifiers are people who "bless" a decision. Most organizations have one or a few people who are called on to say, "Yes, that's a good decision," before it can be carried out. These "elder statesmen/women" seldom have the organizational power of a president or faculty senate leader. Nevertheless, by their character, experience, and presence, they often give authority to a direction. Their hallmark, unlike political or organizational leaders who are powerful influences during the development of a direction, is silence. They are impassive observers. In the end, however, no one feels comfortable until the ratifier's opinion is heard. Although the role seems anachronistic, it is quite amazing how many organizations have such a role.

Understand the power of precedent. While I would, of course, argue that mindlessly following precedent forces the institution to be stuck in the status quo, we should not underestimate the usefulness of precedent to the smooth running of the organization. Mindlessly spouting ad hoc responses to situations is probably the greater evil. Continuing the precedent has the advantages of predictability and silent communication. Because your group has done it this way before, the reactions, necessary conditions, and consequences are pretty well known. Because other groups think you will react this way, there is little need to explicitly warn them of a change.

If you decide to move away from precedent, you have to think a lot harder about reactions and consequences (Cyert and March, 1963, 33–34). If the bursar decides to move the financial suspension date up five days earlier in the semester, the new date may hit the registrar's peak time, and the consequences may be that the suspensions are conducted haphazardly and with great protest from the registrar's office.

The key word, of course, is "mindlessly." We are forced to face decisions to move away from precedent when the environment changes, when we change, and when our strategy changes. Mailing bills home may have worked fine before, but when 5 percent of our students are more than 1,000 miles away, studying at a distance, the effectiveness of this practice must be questioned.

Rumors make decisions. "We're opening a campus in Poindexter City. I heard it from Joe the mailroom guy." Did you ever think that Joe was actually paid by the university's board to test ideas? If there was little negative reaction, they proceeded. I actually don't think this is how it works, but rumors do seem to be like army scouts—looking for trouble, reading the land. Rumor control requires that there be a frequent and dependable source of information about what is going on. To the extent that events are happening in secret, rumors can be damaging, because they spread information without the usual qualifications. The conflict between rumors, the rank-and-file method of reducing uncertainty, and secrecy, the administration's tool to increase control, can be great. A strategic organization will treat rumors as another good source of information, not legitimizing them, but promising to study the idea.

People make decisions in a strategic organization that causes it to do well, not just look good. There are many organizations, especially those that live or die in the political arena, that give people "points" for making decisions that make the organization look good, while ignoring those that could make it do or perform well. Think of the whole chain of events that lead to public organizations needing to spend exactly their budgets. There is no reward for underspending. It's gone. Why? Because it doesn't look good to underspend. That's equivalent to overfunding. That's easy for the legislature to fix. Setting aside funds to make a strategic investment for the future is not an easy practice in these universities.

Being lucky is not equivalent to making a good decision. Betting against the probabilities is a bad decision, even if it turns out okay. Probabilities are always based on the past, so believing that the world has changed, making today's probabilities different, is fine reasoning. Betting against the old probabilities because of new observations can be a good decision.

Likewise, being unlucky against the probabilities (that you still believe are true today) is not evidence of bad decisionmaking. Misestimating the probabilities is evidence of bad decisionmaking. The world rewards the lucky. That can't be helped. One must strive to be correct, nevertheless. While we probably overestimate our powers in producing luck, we probably underestimate its importance. Nevertheless, evolution does seem to rest on the survival of the fittest (those who play the odds correctly) and the lucky.

Aversion to risk varies with possible losses: respect your elders. Although aversion to risk does seem to vary according to certain character traits, the greatest determinant is the level of responsibility for loss. In not-for-profit universities, trustees are responsible by law for the tangible and intangible assets of these public trusts. With that burden of responsibility comes the right of risk determination. These decisions are familiar and definable when a trustee committee sets investment guidelines for an endowment manager. The territory is more unfamiliar to trustees, however, when new financial software is purchased, for example. In either case, however, the decision is strengthened when trustees are assisted in understanding the risks and can help develop guidelines.

Correct decisions are not always good decisions. There are many options that on many scales appear to be correct. If it moves the organization away from its goals, however, the decision is not good. If the decision results in the organization having to violate its values, the organization will be changed and will seem to have lost its way, regardless of its approach to any goals. Abandoning values can only be done slowly and carefully. The additional criteria imposed by the word "good" are that the choice or result of the decision needs to be the option that most efficiently moves the organization toward its goal and that the decision must be such that the organization is able to act in a way that matches its values (Drucker, 2001, 247). This idea will be developed more clearly below.

A good weekly exercise to improve your ability to understand the decisions that are flowing through your organization is to list once a week all decisions that were made and those that were partly made. You will find that the second list is much longer—every week. To get better at recognizing decision opportunities, even those that proceed so slowly that only small steps are visible, begin by putting the decisions into "spheres," like pricing, service, academic core, and so forth. The purpose of this exercise is to recognize what gets decided at your institution and how. Strategic thinking is going to require that you next assess each decision for its potential to further the strategic aims of the university.

A Day in the Life: Susan Goltine, CFO of Surefoot College

Susan sat at her desk, looking out at the deep green of the late spring trees in the foothills of the Alleghenies. The budget was almost done. She and the executive team (affectionately known as the "ET") had slashed and cajoled a gap of $6 million three months ago down to $275,000. Salary increases were not what people had hoped for, but holding the line had helped. Some projects had been deferred—in fact, all projects had been deferred, but core programs were not harmed. No layoffs were necessary and the budget supported four new people: three new faculty members and one secretary for a department that had lost its secretary in the cuts of four years ago.

There was also a little bit of stretching of revenue estimates, but early signs looked good. There had been no drop in applications, and expectations were high for the new emphasis on retention. Surely the bright talk on the campus on "student-centeredness" and "bold, intrusive measures" to stem disaffection with the college would have an effect on a retention rate that should not be hard to improve.

She stared at the nearly completed budget. From the corner of her eye, she saw the photo of her husband and young daughter and, distracted, thought, "Soon, darlings, I will have weekends again." She took a deep breath, and began thinking out loud, "I'll take $150,000 from library acquisitions. I'll remove the part-time assistant from my office. That should quiet them. I think I can add $25,000 to gift revenue and take $35,000 from advertising. They should not have expected that increase anyway. I'll then just have to ask the provost to take $25,000 out of various supply budgets, and I'm done, except for running it by the ET."

She put new numbers in her spreadsheet, using a dummy academic account for the supplies reduction, and printed out the summary. She then prepared an e-mail to the ET announcing the final result and requesting that a final budget discussion be added to tomorrow's meeting agenda and attached the summary.

She looked out her window and saw that the sun had disappeared behind the western hills, but a few trees higher up were bathed in light at their tops. She could see the light too, at the end of the tunnel, but she still faced budget "town halls," meetings with vice presidents, budget letters, press releases, discussions on the tuition increase, board meetings, and preparation of the budget numbers for loading into the computer. Nevertheless, she felt she could relax a little now.

Susan reflected back on the last few weeks. How had they found the $6 million? The gap had seemed so impossible three months ago, while also seeming familiar and normal. She had been a CFO for eight years now, and the big cycles were getting pretty much routine. Every year the library acquisitions budget was set in the last stages to match what was available. Noncritical deferred maintenance projects disappeared in the second round. She had been forced into the increase in faculty. Faculty recruiting decisions had to be made long before she could prepare revenue estimates. The new recruiting and retention initiatives had made everyone optimistic last spring, before the fall enrollment numbers came in. Then Professors Pierce and Hayden had not retired as the rumors had predicted, and there they were: three new faculty members with appointment letters in hand and no one out the door.

The tuition decision took a more interesting path. Back in December she had proposed 6 percent in her first, rough revenue forecast. The college had gone with 7 percent last year, and she thought the reaction had been pretty strong from students, and even from some members of the board. She just called it a "working number." The enrollment management VP proposed a zero increase, but no one took him seriously. The president threw out 10 percent, just to see what the reaction would be. The president justified the idea, because, she said, "It showed our commitment to excellence." Nevertheless, Susan guessed the board had not encouraged the idea later.

After several weeks, Susan saw the 6 percent figure in other places. The faculty budget committee asked for a discussion of it. The financial aid office prepared some estimates of the impact on student aid packages (and, in fact, showed that most of the revenue increase would go to funding higher packages). When she did the draft budget in January, she continued to use 6 percent, because no one really had objected. Later, in February, the recruiting coordinator showed how a 6 percent increase kept them relatively in line with their competitors (excluding the state institutions), and a 6 percent increase kept the tuition price just under $20,000, which the recruiting office regarded as a psychological barrier.

"And no one thanked me for setting tuition," she thought. "No one even knows where the number came from. I really don't."

Just then the phone rang. "That must be Bill," she mused.

"Hi, Honey. Are you thinking about coming home tonight?" the receiver purred.

"Thinking about it . . ." she laughed.

Seven Key Thoughts

1. Many procedures, policies, mission elements, and strategies have no "original decision maker"—they just "happen."

2. If the "right" people repeat an idea often enough, it magically becomes a decision. The history of a decision is often the record of influence within an organization.

3. A "good" decision is one that moves an organization closer to what is defined as "the desirable future." Has the organization moved? Is the direction strategic?

4. Decisions gravitate toward those willing to make them. Decisions are affected by gravitational pull. The strength of a person's gravitational field is partially determined by his or her apparent willingness to make decisions. This is his or her "decision mass."

5. Decision avoidance signals an unwillingness to participate in strategic change. While not deciding can be called deciding (but without contemplation), not searching for decision opportunities is a greater compound sin. It is sloth mixed with cowardice.

6. All decisions are "gut" decisions. They differ in how well informed one's "gut" is. Listen to your "gut," but never stop gathering data.

7. Decide when one must—just in time. To decide too early is to chance the loss of information. Events never stop happening. Some of them may help inform your decision.

Chapter Five
COMMON PRACTICES IN PRIORITIZING PROJECTS

Many influences on the priorities we set in choosing projects and alternatives, such as affordability, the choices of competitors, time constraints, and the source of the proposed choices, may result in less-than-optimal movement toward our vision. But we can move decisionmaking into a strategic context, where we need to understand and swear off our dependence on the traditional contexts.

One of the finest products of current strategic planning efforts is a set of institutional priorities (Rowley and Sherman, 2001, 201). When influencing the direction of an institution, few things convey more in fewer words than a set of priorities. The scarcest resource of a university is administrative time, more so than money. While more money can buy a bit more time, the return from 5 percent more administrative time will be far greater than 5 percent more in the budget. That is why priorities are so critical.

RATIONALES FOR CURRENT PROJECT CHOICE

Can we afford it? The criterion of affordability is not without merit, but it must be applied with considerable sophistication. If the criterion is whether or not the project can be fit into the budget, then the choice of projects is strongly biased toward the status quo. If strategies are not driving the budget, then the status quo is driving the institution.

A more productive set of financial questions than simply "Can we afford it" includes: "Is the return from the investment in this project, both financial and nonfinancial, greater than all other possible investments when viewed with an understanding of the risks? Is there a way to finance this project that does not change the costs and risks so much that other projects become better choices? And, can this project be timed to improve the return and financing opportunities?" These questions on rate of return, financing options, and timing are certainly more difficult than determining if the project fits into the budget. If the return on the investment is too low, the risks are too great, the financing is too costly or improbable, or the timing cannot be managed, then it may be deemed unaffordable.

Budgets can be used as shields for the status quo, or they can be used to free resources from tiring efforts for brighter prospects. "We can't afford it" is armor for the status quo.

Isn't everybody else doing it? These are defensive moves. Our competitors have adopted a new technology, a new scholarship program, or more colorful advertisements, and we must follow suit. Do you remember wiring whole buildings for "educational TV"? Keeping Division I athletics at a loss of $7 million per year? How about the scholarship wars and the Campaigns for Everyone?

If your strategy is to look exactly like your competitors, then this is an excellent criterion. If your strategy is designed to give you an edge through a unique approach, this criterion had better be dropped (Cohen and March, 1974, 224). At least your university should modify the question to: How can we do *it* in a way that makes us unique and pushes us toward our goals?

The wildfire spread of technological innovation can sometimes be problematic. For example, barcode checkout of books seems very elegant, but it probably saves graduate students 35 seconds per book. It did make our graduate schools look just like the mega-universities but staff had to be added to maintain the system at considerable cost. Conversely, real search advances came with the introduction of online card catalogs.

Following the crowd is not the problem. It's the fear of being perceived as different. Fear is an unfortunate motivator. The best criteria for project selection are positive.

Who has the time? The criterion of time constraints reveals the paradox of this way of thinking. If we had time, we would not need priorities. The lack of time only presses the need to use true criteria to help choose the most important things to do. The manager who has no time to hire an assistant is the manager who has lost sight of priorities. Most often this is a "latent" criterion. It is the reason why the project was never started, never implemented. The "on paper" priority may have been high, but the implementation priority may have been zero.

While some of the blame for invoking this inappropriate criterion can be placed on a manager's shortsighted vision, much may be placed on the project development process. Projects are often developed and evaluated with overly optimistic ideas about resource requirements. For example, believing that staffing at the current level is sufficient to implement a new student information system software package can cripple implementation. Expecting staff members to do their current jobs, learn a new system, test installations, set requirements, clean transfer data, set switches, and input missing data is equivalent to requesting resistance. When a new project is given a high priority but the choice is made in ignorance of the true cost, why should a team approach it with anything but reluctance? Unless the staff in our software implementation example is supplemented with temporary workers who can do major parts of existing jobs, that staff really does not have the time to implement the program.

Whose idea was it? While we know that ideas from the president and the board should come from a strategic framework, the building of that web of rationale is as important as the authority of the origin. Likewise, when ideas are ignored because they do not come from the opinion leaders of the organization, the organization is unlikely to sustain sufficient growth to remain successful. The culture of disaster reputed to have crept into NASA is one where lower-echelon engineers who saw problems were silenced.

GOOD RULES FOR BAD PROJECTS

A number of flawed "rules," such as avoidance, failure to validate, pigeon holing, lack of ongoing reevaluation, emphasizing quantity over quality, and favoritism are traditionally used to develop priorities and to manage projects. These practices have arisen because of the lack of time we all face. They are the easy way out. They make life easier in the short run but harder in the long run. They slow the movement of the institution toward its vision.

You can list everyone's projects (but you manage by ignoring most). This is a political stratagem that allows you to stay in everyone's favor. Keep a very public list. Don't give priorities. Begin implementation of a couple of projects and tell everyone else that theirs is just around the corner. Of course, this method doesn't survive a call for an explanation of priorities.

Cost estimates and timelines are the last thing you do. This is fairly common. After getting strong commitment for an idea, you then do the calculations that show how terribly expensive and difficult the project will be. Done correctly, even a rough cost estimate at the beginning can help focus priority setting. Too often projects that should die early are allowed to live because of the "tremendous investment we have already put in." That, of course, is a violation of the principle of sunk costs. (Decisions should never be made on costs already incurred. Decisions must only be based on the future marginal costs and benefits of each alternative. No matter which alternative is selected, previous costs can never be reversed.) Getting early cost estimates also forces proponents to sharpen their benefit calculations and estimates. Getting a favorable reception for a "costless" project is not terribly difficult.

All projects must fall into at least one of the college's broad, strategic themes: quality, access, diversity, and technology. While I am a strong proponent of using strategic priorities to determine project priorities, the strategic priorities must be grounded and meaningful. The kinds of priorities in the rule above are so general that any project can find shelter under one of the umbrellas (Schaffer, 1992, 83).

We can stop planning now because we don't have the resources to add any more projects. This rule is a symptom of the inability to say no to a project. This rule gives you a way to say no: first come; first served. Project ranking should be a continuous process. As new project ideas come along, as priorities shift, and as new cost and benefit information becomes available, project priorities should be reevaluated.

The measure of a good plan is the number of projects it contains. A large number may be a good starting point. Nevertheless, the measure of a good plan is the quality of the projects as measured by their ability to move the institution forward strategically. A large number of projects generally indicates that priorities have not been developed. As noted above, the inability to cull may stem from a reluctance to say no, from a lack of good cost and benefit information, or from a lack of careful specification of strategic priorities.

The best way to get a committee to function is to pay each member off by giving a high priority to his or her area's favorite project. Well, it *is* one way to get the strategic planning committee to function. It is also a good way to ensure meeting attendance and a strong volunteer rate for the committee. It may also be good for a number of individuals' vision, but not the institution's vision.

This quick look at problems with some common approaches to project development shows that it clearly is possible to fail at project development, and it should sensitize the reader to common difficulties. Chapter 11 of this book describes a process that assigns the development of strategies widely across the organization as a part of daily activities. A key piece of strategy development is the creation of strategic metrics that can be used to evaluate the degree that projects move the institution within its strategies toward its vision. Requiring strategic justifications for projects would end many of the ills described in the paragraphs above.

A Day in the Life: Mary-Gold Billings, Vice President of Planning, Nanterre State University

MG, as she had always been called, walked from her building at the edge of campus to the administration building. Although everyone seemed to agree that she should have an office in this building, none was vacant and nothing had changed in the two years since she had been hired. The campus planning office had found a nice space for her in the dean for humanities suite, and, although she had to make the long walk across campus several times a day, she usually did not mind. The Midwestern day was heating up, but the many young maples provided a bit of shade as she walked.

Today she was to meet with the executive staff and present the planning task force steering committee's final project list for the next five years. She wondered how the president would react to this $87 million list. She had completed the list, fitted all the projects onto a five-year timeline, worked with the finance office on budgets for each one, listed project outcomes, and named teams responsible for each project.

She had built widespread support for the projects with more than 125 people on the project task forces. The faculty had been particularly receptive to working with her. The steering committee had worked on ideas from 10 teams, each focused on a different "key point of success" of the strategic plan. She had assistance from IT on the design of a Web site where faculty, students, staff, and even alumni could read planning document drafts, see the project designs taking shape, and register ideas and comments. It had been a massive undertaking with the project plans alone filling 154 pages. Fortunately, everything was online, so she only had to carry her laptop with her.

Just then she heard her name and turned to see Dr. William Black, the CFO, huffing to catch up with her. "Hi, Dr. Bill," she greeted him as most people did.

"Hi, MG," he returned. "I've been preparing for the unveiling. I'll walk with you to the execution." His black humor was his trademark.

"Bill, I'm really looking forward to this. I think we have the makings of a new university here."

"Just kidding." He smiled. "We all admire your work." He paused, then went on, "You know, however, those numbers have gotten a little scary. Where am I going to find $87 million?"

"You always take things so personally."

"I'm doing the looking, right?"

"Yes, but the legislature and education staff pushed the idea of planning and got me hired. The money comes from them, not you," she said, trying to take off some of the "air of heavy responsibility" that Bill always carried. "Besides, the plan only requires $7 million in the first year. Timing is everything."

"Well, I'm not sure that the legislature was equating planning with spending $87 million, and there are some projects I am not sure have been thought through very well, besides." With the sun in his eyes, he was having trouble keeping a scowl off his face. He liked MG and knew that her work was necessary.

"Like what?" she said, trying not to sound defensive, but, in fact, failing.

"Well, take the renovations to the science labs, for example. That's a big chunk of dough—technical accounting term," he said, winking and trying to lighten the mood a little. "I don't know where we will teach science during the three years of the renovations. Those old buildings really don't have the infrastructure to support new labs. Besides, I've been reading about some schools that are using technology to teach labs. I've read about some places having success even with distance learning using virtual labs."

"Distance learning," she replied. "That's another initiative, and the president strongly supports us moving in that direction. Don't forget, if we don't upgrade our labs, our teachers won't find jobs. High schools have better labs than we do."

"I suppose, but I can't help but wonder how much of this $87 million we will see in five years," he said as they turned into the relative gloom of the administration building foyer.

Noting a sign on the silver doors of the elevator, she said, "Looks like we climb today. I guess I would vote for an elevator that actually worked over a new science lab."

Bill rolled his eyes, "Now you're talking."

Seven Key Thoughts

1. Priority support for a project with no clear connection to the future of the organization gets tainted with the description, "It's political." There is always a danger that the whole planning enterprise can be condemned when there is no transparent rationale for why projects gain favor and make progress.

2. Too often project priorities are determined by the fear that someone else is doing something flashy, and we will lose the race if we don't do the same. There is no harm in not doing something that doesn't fit our own strategies.

3. Our gift to the next generation of decisionmakers will not be our projects, but a better understanding of how to select projects. Improvements to the project prioritization process will come slowly. Understanding and clarifying priorities will take some time. Skills in developing costs and benefits are slowly won. A smooth process brings many benefits, generating not only better priorities, but also better ideas for projects. As the process for project development and ranking becomes clearer, the incentives for developing projects also become clearer.

4. Project selection often resembles candidate selection: any blemish kills a chance, regardless of overall merit. This is almost a definition of mediocrity. Only the most mediocre projects survive a beauty contest. Rather than combine values for multidimensional assessments, eliminating a project with a blemish indiscriminately removes good projects with correctable flaws or with flaws that are more than offset by advantages.

5. The project development process and the budget development process must be integrated. A budget is a formal presentation of project priority, and funding projects is the ultimate expression of priority.

6. A budget with no funding for new activities is an expression of the priority of not changing direction—the preference for drift. To develop project plans and then not to fund them is evidence of the lack of a link between planning and budgeting.

7. Support from the top is critical to establishing project priorities (and is critical to legitimizing "the top"), but the support must be reasoned. Handpicking projects by the president or board short-circuits the process. The projects should flow from presidentially endorsed strategic institutional priorities. Universities should avoid reversing the process.

Chapter Six

WHEN PLANNING GETS IN THE WAY OF DOING

The project-oriented approach to planning that is often used by universities today has both strengths and weaknesses. The current methodologies do permit us to step outside of and evaluate current practice, to meet and enlist new people who can bring new insights to the process, and to learn and understand the thinking of the leaders of the institution. But the process often fails to integrate smoothly with decisionmaking.

CURRENT PLANNING PROCESS STRENGTHS

Countering the failures of current management. Emergencies often bend our sight toward the short run. Planning asks that we think about the future. In the best of planning circumstances we ask, "What do we know about the future based on trends and our knowledge of other impending changes that require advance preparation? What are the opportunities? What are the challenges?"

Daily work life requires that we concentrate very strongly on the trees and ignore the forest. Individual problems, petitions, exceptions, failures, and faulty systems require constant attention. We manage offices and interactions but rarely concern ourselves with the momentum of the organization as a whole. CFOs do pay attention to the whole institution's fiscal solvency, but they rarely have a chance to view the university as an organic whole over other dimensions.

Our focus on our classes, our students, our processes, our people, and our computers keeps us from examining much beyond our walls. Rarely do we give competitors a second thought. We often dismiss them on the grounds of trivial differences between our programs. Differences that we clearly see, but that our future students may not find terribly interesting. We rarely acknowledge that we compete against the armed services, entrepreneurialism, and alternative lifestyles. We barely recognize the other colleges and universities that draw students who might be ours. Porter (1996b, 39) cautions not to equate operational effectiveness with strategy. We must not fixate on life within the university, discounting competition and other external events.

Porter (1996a, 22) also describes the goal of the strategist as positioning his or her institution in a way that helps the institution best defend itself against the bargaining power of suppliers and customers and the threat of "new entrants" into the market, including "substitute products." "Position" is the key metaphor. We are looking for the "place," described in terms of price, product, perception, and value, where the university is more effective than its competitors. Finding that place is the topic of much of this book.

Planning often provides the opportunity to realistically assess our competition, not just competition for students, but also competition for a range of resources. Planning often includes fact-gathering periods when competitive academic programs, prices, and student numbers are discovered and put into perspective. Occasionally, these exercises use focus groups to identify the characteristics the general public assigns to our university and to our competitors. This gives our "position" in terms of our competition. These revelations can help the institution focus its appeal and give it incentives for improving areas that appear weak to the outside world. Often the perception of the outside world is more correct than we are willing to admit.

Strategic planning counters the tendency to focus on internal operations and helps remind us that we are service organizations. We exist to serve our publics, especially our students. Strategic planning forces us to think of our operations in terms of our mission. Missions emphasize whom we serve. The challenges we face can be overcome by improving the services we provide—and becoming better than our competitors.

Meet new people. No sarcasm intended. People join planning task forces from across the university. This is part of what helps give participants a clearer view of the organization as a whole (Cohen and March, 1974, 115). These relationships foster cooperation across the organization later. Planning allows the synergies that are possible when people with different backgrounds and strengths get together.

Find out what the president thinks is really important. Okay, there's a little sarcasm here. Presidents do use the planning process as a forum for their views. In good situations, the president also listens carefully and improves his or her views with new ideas. Chapter 12 will note when and where leadership is most critical to the process of planning, and where the leader should take a step back.

Get my projects listed as important things to do. The final sarcasm, I promise.

POSITIVE RESULTS FROM CURRENT PLANNING PROCESSES

Mission. Most planning exercises begin with a focus on the mission (Karol and Ginsburg, 1980, 220). Questions of whom the university serves are reviewed. Proper wording is pored over and tweaks are made. Often the mission exercise is combined with a general realignment of slogan, logo, stationery, and mascot. The slogan is an external message. The mission should be internal. It does not have to list everything that is worthy about the institution, because it is an internal focus point. It should precisely state why the institution exists. Whom does it serve? What is distinctive about it that makes it important to its clientele?

Most institutions that begin a strategic planning exercise with a mission exploration end up affirming their existing mission. Crisis may force the abandonment of a historic mission, as when the enrollments and finances of a single-sex institution force reevaluation. Usually, however, the task force that pursues the task of examining and evaluating the mission gives all members of the community a deeper understanding of the institution's role and reason for being. The effort becomes a celebration of the mission. Newer faculty and staff may gain energy and commitment from the process of reaffirming the institution's role, as defined by founders and carried on by current leaders.

Sometimes the charge of the mission task force is to consolidate five or six mission statements that have grown up for different purposes. There is the "old" mission statement, the mission as presented by the athletic department, a mission statement crafted for a capital campaign, and the mission statement that happens to be printed in the catalog. Probably all overlap a great deal and certainly all have a ring of truth. The exercise of narrowing the field and affirming a single statement requires a bit of pruning and digging for what is vital about the university.

In almost all cases the institution can claim that the focus, the understanding of purpose, and the commonality of language justifies the two and one-half years of deliberation by a group of distinguished philosophy, physics, and English professors (Dolence, Rowley and Lujan, 1997, 139).

Action plans. Action plans are the deliverable of most strategic planning exercises. These plans include projects that must be undertaken (as I mentioned above), research studies that should be conducted, and staffing levels to ensure success. In a few cases these strategic planning action plans differ little from day-to-day operational plans. Usually, however, they represent efforts the institution must undertake to better meet the future. Unlike day-to-day operational plans, they are not made in response to an immediate problem or emergency. The best action plans each have a future justification.

Many techniques have been used to generate action plans. Sometimes committees are charged with doing so and rely on the ingenuity of committee members. Sometimes the administration holds a retreat for campus leaders and facilitators assist the group in envisioning the future and winnowing long lists of ideas to a manageable set. Sometimes a planning task force designs a "bottom up" technique, where departments each develop a plan, including action plans. These departmental plans are welded into divisional plans and then compaction finally yields the grand institutional plan.

The mark of success of these action plans is that a number of the efforts listed are actually carried out and benefit the university. Many institutions can point with pride to a system implementation, an academic realignment, a revised registration process, or a campus renewal effort that gained impetus during strategic planning and dominated a list of action plans.

Such action plans rarely seem to rise to the level of strategic efforts, however. That is, the methodology does not seem to imbed the actions in any sort of coherent strategic framework. These shortcomings are discussed in chapter 5.

Multilevel thinking. The intellectual framework given in the figures in chapter 2 demonstrates the many levels of thought required in an effort to direct change in an institution. Pieces of a number of the levels come into play with the present processes when an institution engages in planning, and the higher levels of mission and vision are engaged. A much more concrete level of actions is pursued with project lists, and concepts are more deeply explored as in the 1970s when Stanford's planning effort led to a full exploration of the meaning of financial equilibrium and intergenerational equity.

The greatest gain for the organization, however, is not in having people make progress at several levels of thought, but in assisting organizational members to recognize that other people in the organization operate at different levels. We have all too often seen one person bring up what that person believes to be an important principle, only to have another person disagree strongly by stating an operational activity. The activity may or may not be conceivable within the scope of the principle. In most cases, it is unrelated. The two people, however, end up talking completely past each other, more absorbed in the apparent disagreement than the fact that one has an abstract point to make and the other a concrete point. Planning exercise facilitators spend much time disentangling these near misses. Facilitators who fail to keep discussion at the same level of abstraction of either "What are our principles?" or "What projects must we undertake to fulfill these principles?" will see discussion bogging down. An awareness of these levels is often gained through planning projects.

STUMBLING BLOCKS TO EFFECTIVE PLANNING

Many university strategic plans are doomed to failure. Consider, for example, the five-year plan that has spent 18 months to 2 years with several committees, guided by a steering committee. The plan may then be "reviewed" every year until the fifth year, when a "plan to plan" is begun, but put off for several years, waiting for the new president to initiate. The annual reviews generally consist of progress reports on the list of projects enumerated in the original plan, usually augmented by new projects added by the president's cabinet. The pathologies to watch out for are the following:

Lack of sustained attention to the future. Many planning projects do a good job of assessing job opportunities for graduates, state funding prospects, and even future high school graduate pools from feeder high schools. Much of the planning, unfortunately, is based on straight-line projections of two- or three-year trends. This look into the future through the course of the five years of implementation is often not sustained. Shifts in demographics, strengthening or weakening economies, immigration trends, and changes in relationships with feeder schools are noticed only by luck. The people who were assigned the task of assessing future prospects during the planning project go back to their "regular work" when the project is completed.

Insufficient attention to the needs of "customers." Another thing to watch out for is too little attention to students and other served constituencies and too much attention to the internal affairs of the university. What is the purpose of a new student system, if students are not better served? Adding another faculty member to the history department would improve the department, but who is served? If student success is part of the mission, have we defined what we mean by "student success?" What are we doing to assure it?

This weakness is being addressed by greater attention to assessment. How do we know we are actually succeeding at our mission? How much can we measure? Can we measure student success? Can we measure the contribution toward student success of each of our planning ventures?

Denial of the existence of competitors. I have found that many institutions believe being unique allows them to ignore competition. The only college for women in the northern part of the state may believe that they only have a bit of competition with a similar institution in the southern part of the state. The English department, with its emphasis on literature, may be unique, but a more operational term is "different." Too many colleges take an "inside" point of view instead of the point of view of a potential student, potential donor, or the legislature. To a potential student, the "only women's college in our state" is only a choice. The potential student is not just choosing among women's colleges, but among many colleges, especially the very competitive public universities in the area. The English department's ability to differentiate itself works only with fairly sophisticated viewers. To an outsider, it's just an English department.

Institutions react with surprise and shame when they find that the main characteristic differentiating them from their competitors is a reputation as a party school. A successful strategic plan includes careful focus group evaluations of the word-of-mouth reputations among potential constituencies. The institution must then decide whether to enhance, repudiate, or manage "party school," "bad dorm," or "quiet" images. Few universities, however, successfully manage or project as part of their image the real transformations they create in students any further than suggesting that a degree is the key to a better life.

The degree, however, is the same value that most competitors present as well. What differentiates colleges is the nature of the transformation. Too few institutions understand the strengths of their transformation and seek to enhance those strengths. An important strategic emphasis is the decision to present certain successful transformations to potential students. Any institution can sell a student a degree and a good time. Not all institutions can help a student transform into a success.

Transformations include developing academic skills. Institutions are doing much better at establishing minimum levels of competency for these types of skills. In addition, institutions change attitudes. They can give students attitudes that lead to success, like an understanding of and a readiness to make decisions. Institutions also give students skills to be successful in complex environments by simulating those complexities.

Along the dimension of transformation, a LaGuardia Community College (LCC) can compete with a Harvard. LCC can be excellent in the types of transformations it achieves. It competes well with Harvard in doing so. A potential student has a choice between the two. LCC may offer that student a superior transformation. This is a strategic recognition of competition as helping to define success. LCC competes with Hostos and with Queens College. It must define its transformation set with sufficient clarity that it can demonstrate why, for a large group of potential students, it offers the best chance for a transformation that spells success for that group. It must also manage those transformations such that it really does become excellent at doing so.

Lack of in-depth treatment of the effect of changing technologies. Planning processes seem to have trouble striking a balance between ignorance of changes in technology on educational and administrative processes and putting technology on an uncritical pedestal. While distance learning is not a modality that is necessary for all institutions, many have been slow to assist students with online syllabi and homework submission. Conversely, justifying every budget request that includes the word "technology" is hardly strategic either.

Technology is merely a tool that has the potential to assist an institution in furthering its strategic goals. I think we have finally begun to realize that technology is not an end in itself.

Lack of strategies. What? No strategies in strategic plans? A strategy can be characterized as an organizing theme around which change can occur. A strategy says, "Here are our publics (markets, potential students, donors, legislators) and here is how we are going to increase their allegiance to us over our competitors, those who would also like to serve them." Too many plans describe no direction of change for the institution, no way of confronting the environment, no declaration of advantage.

Some plans are not meant to be strategic. These plans celebrate the status quo. Some "tweaking" is suggested, but no unifying theme of change is sounded. To the degree the environment is static, these plans may be sufficiently strategic to maintain success.

Some plans are all about change but have no theme. These plans have long lists of projects and demonstrate a belief that the university must be all things to all people. The theme is "do everything now."

Some plans lay a good groundwork for a strategy but then avoid pulling it together. The university that has special scholarships for valedictorians and sees itself as just below the "Ivies" just cannot bring itself to admit that its transformations are really most beautiful for bright, but perhaps initially self-effacing, blue-collar kids.

Some plans come up with a strategy that no one believes. We all remember the variations on "the Harvard of New York."

Lack of value exploration. A large number of college and university Web sites clearly and carefully display institutional values. What is missing on these Web sites is a process of engaging values to see how they apply to actual decision situations and real strategies. This process often reveals gaps in stated values. There are many unwritten guides to action that only become evident during a process of exploration and attempted application.

A huge range of possible values exists. Complete this sentence: "I am really comfortable working for X University because they really believe in. . . ." How strongly does your institution believe in employee development? What is your employee education budget? How strongly do you believe in opportunities for the disabled? Has someone gone through all job descriptions to edit out those less-than-necessary requirements that block the hiring of a disabled person? Can a person make a mistake and recover? (See Rowley and Sherman (2001, 307–8) for the role of error in strategic choice.) What broader roles do you play in your community? How is volunteer work made possible?

Sophisticated strategies relate to values. They also help define "how" a strategy is to be pursued, that is, in what way. The process is simultaneous and iterative. Strategies suggest where values should be honed. Values suggest limits and strengths in strategies. For example, a university with a strategy to bring higher education to working adults that also values a role in its communities must think deeply about how distance education can foster community improvement. The strength of the strategy may be just that nexus. Developing projects and credit assignments that bring students at a distance into their communities could be a point of distinction.

Lack of methods for developing concepts. Institutions need to foster increased understanding of what they do. Teaching, learning, surviving as economic entities; passing on structures and knowledge to future generations; and adding to knowledge are all things that institutions do. A competent strategic plan will lay out a methodology for discovering and distributing core concepts. For example, every day someone generates new research on learning. How will this learning-based organization evaluate and disseminate that research?

Lack of sound principles. The intellectual framework that holds strategies, values, and vision together is a set of simplifying abstract statements that tell what an institution stands for, where it is going, and how it is going to get there. For example: "This university will achieve national recognition for its success in bringing high-risk students through its universal guided-student teams to graduation with no decrease in the current excellence of all academic programs." This is the rallying cry. The strategy itself must define "high risk," "teams," and "excellence." This principle states a piece of the vision, a key strategy, and an important value. Now we must develop the strategy further. How will we fund this initiative? What is it about excellent academic programs that we value? How are we going to continuously improve our understanding of what works for high-risk student retention? How are we going to make the budget trade-off between the proportion of students that we accept as high risk and the cost of our retention investments?

The principle is the broad, unifying statement. The development of principles is a first step that too many strategic plans skip.

Current strategic planning processes foster a static view. The "end" of the process is sought, not a process for operating every day. The set of values or the list of projects is viewed as an end point, not the process for continually refining values and evaluating projects (Cohen and March, 1974, 221). How can we learn to value the journey, not the document?

We emphasize the vision, not methods for refining, discussing, and sharing the vision. We stumble to the finish line, document in hand, with too little breath to ask, "How can we improve?"

Current strategic planning processes do not foster a search for opportunities. Too often the prescription is too tight: first we will do this, then this, then this, and finally this! When a new opportunity is seen, we seem to fear the criticism, "We can't do that. It's not in the plan." We can't seem to say, "Our strategy is roughly in this direction. Raises and trophies to those who can figure out and implement things that kind of fit." This is one of the primary differences between a strategic plan and a strategic attitude.

A Day in the Life: Jill Fierengelli, Associate VP for Finance, Devonshire University

Dr. Fierengelli sat at her desk in her tiny office in the treasurer's suite of offices on the seventh floor of the university's main administration building, Muir Hall. She was a reader, and books lined the walls of the windowless office and were piled in stacks on the floor. She had lately been reading much about strategic planning and organizational behavior. Her doctorate had been in educational administration. She had recently been asked to lead a group to "take strategic planning at DU to a higher level." Her hands rested on the keyboard of her computer, but they were not moving.

"We've accomplished a lot in the last two years," she thought, "but what's missing?" She recalled the work that had been done to sharpen the mission statement, targeting students in the five-state area who desired an education, preparing them for leadership. The statement was also broadened to include education for adults, moving to leadership positions in their workplaces and communities. This was a tremendous shift, in fact, away from a supposed national audience and education for education's sake.

The university president had then led a process to identify projects likely to foster this new mission. A total of 50 projects had been culled from a starting list of 230. A task force had identified initiatives for further development in distance education, a new educational administration degree program to train principals and superintendents, a new student union, an expanded new-employee orientation, new computer laboratories, and many other projects. For each of the projects, budgets were developed, timelines were stretched, and project leaders were identified.

Nevertheless, when the revised mission and project plans were presented to the trustees as a strategic plan, one vocal member of the board planning subcommittee, who was the president of a large multinational corporation, said, "That was a lot of work. Where's the strategy?" The president indicated that the plan was a "living document" and that any missing sections would be filled in later. That was now Jill's task.

She had to admit that the trustee had a good point. It did seem that they had jumped from the mission to projects rather glibly. She also knew that the head of the trustee finance committee had "found it difficult to see the connection between the proposed budget and the plan." The president had pointed out several places where the budget had start-up costs for several of the projects, but this trustee persisted, pointing out that little else in the budget could be justified by the plan.

"What would justify the budget, including funding for continuing programs, administrative expenses, salary increases, the tuition increase, and revisions to the financial aid structure?" she mused. "Does the plan have to justify window replacement in the dorms and the new staff assistant for political science? That doesn't make sense."

From her reading, she had developed a fairly strong idea of what a strategy was. She decided to outline her thoughts. As she began outlining, she realized she was developing a charge for the new task force she would lead. She listed these questions to be answered:

"What business are we in?

What businesses could we be in?

Whom do we serve?

Who competes with us to serve these groups?

What values, ways of doing things, really make us unique?

What competitive advantages and disadvantages do we have against each competitor?

How do we increase advantages and decrease disadvantages?

How would we know if we were successful in five years?

What do we as an organization know too little about?"

As she crafted these questions, she thought about how to move toward answers in a way that the entire campus community would hear the ideas and witness the movement toward a more unified set of answers. She picked up the phone and called the chief information officer.

"Venkatesh here."

"Venkie, this is Jill. I would like to spend some time with you talking about ways I can use technology to further the strategic planning work I'm doing now. I need to keep the ideas in front of the community, like on a web page, and I need ways that the task forces can keep discussions going online, like we are doing with our distance education courses."

"That sounds like fun. How about two o'clock tomorrow? My office."

"That works for me."

"Great. See you then. Bye."

"Thanks. Bye."

She hoped she could keep the groups from getting badly bogged down. Her goal was to have them develop a rich set of ideas as answers to the specific questions. If she could just keep them away from long discussions on "My Favorite Solution," they would develop a more detailed vision of the university they believed was necessary for the future.

A healthy set of answers to this first set of questions would allow the steering committee to develop a list of strategic directions the president could develop into a strategic statement. To move from the vision to specific strategies and to tie the strategies to current decisions, she thought of another set of questions that would help frame the discussion.

"How do we develop and recognize opportunities that improve our advantages, lower our disadvantages, and reach more of the people we are dedicated to serve?

What is blocking us from finding opportunities and assisting our target audiences better?

What are the big ideas that define "the right direction"?

What processes do we need to have in place to find and take advantage of opportunities?

What processes do we need to have in place to find and overcome blocks?"

The final piece the task force would need to develop, given some answers to these questions, would be a way to justify and present budgets, she thought. She could see that a series of statements that defined "the right direction," the strategic direction for the college, could be held up as requirements. Each area, project, or initiative would have to be justified in terms of these statements.

"Oh dear," she thought. "How can I keep the development of the strategic directions from becoming a completely parochial exercise? If each person on the task force knows they will have to justify their area and budget in terms of contributions to moving the university in 'the right direction,' they will build 'directions' to fit. I'm not going to lie down on the tracks. I'm going to have to make sure that the president and executive staff understand the need for strong leadership to prevent a runaway train."

Jill looked through the screens she had been developing. "Dear, dear," she thought. "This is a mess. I've got a lot more to do." She could feel her mind shutting down. She saved her work, printed it out, and backed it up. She then locked out her computer, put away the apple that she had forgotten to eat, and stood up. As she turned out the lights, she thought, "Am I going in the right direction on this?"

Deep in thought, she walked toward the elevator.

Seven Key Thoughts

1. Planning is the "work around" we have developed for pulling ourselves away from the fray of day-to-day work and thinking a bit about the future. We seek a context for the decisions we make during the day, but lack the discipline to look for the future on the fly.

2. Strategic planning exercises are not without successes: institutional mission can be carefully assessed, long lists of "necessary" projects, each with its own set of goals and responsible people are made, and successful relationships among people who do not normally work together are cemented. University Web sites are good places to go to look for evidence of strategic planning. Lists of values and departmental priorities can often be found there. Mission statements are almost always present.

3. Strategic planning exercises must have strategic results. The end result must be a sense of shared organizational direction: an idea of what must be done, and what should not be done. The goal of both strategic planning and strategic thinking is the development of a shared sense of direction among organizational members.

4. Strategic planning exercises also often fail to inform concrete daily business, like making budgets. The test, however, of strategic planning is whether any decisions seem to be affected by the process or results. Is there evidence the budget is different because of the plan? Is there evidence the institution understands its environment better?

5. To the extent that the result of a planning exercise stifles creativity, causes the avoidance of opportunities, and decreases critical thinking about the direction and purpose of an institution, it fails. Plans are static. Strategic thought is dynamic.

6. Planning should not be a separate exercise from doing. The two must be carefully meshed and interactive. When a decision opportunity arises, planning has been a failure if you think, "What does the plan say is the answer?" Planning is a success if you think, "What have I learned from the planning process that can help me make this decision?"

7. A plan's beauty is not like that of a statue, to be seen alone, but like that of the sun, for what it illuminates. Illumination in this sense comes in many forms. The illumination of understanding the university's direction. The illumination of understanding that university values proscribe certain approaches. The illumination that the mission requires more thought to cover this situation.

Chapter Seven

THE PLACE OF VALUES
IN STRATEGIC THOUGHT

Values describe how things are done when implementing critical ideas for guiding decisions and organizational behavior that are not so much goal oriented, as they are process oriented. As part of strategic thinking, values help give context to every-day decisions.

The number of institutions that now display institutional values on their Web sites is quite gratifying. These Web pages are a sign that the timing of this book is good. Colleges and universities are grasping the importance of presenting decision context in a public, and certainly campus-wide, manner. While most values presentations are thoughtful and unique to the institution, they generally lack a sense of development or an opportunity for ongoing discussion. The values are presented as unassailable and not to be discussed or debated. This lack of development means that the possibility of increasingly sophisticated explication is lost. Nevertheless, wearing "your values on your sleeve" integrates the community and improves daily decisions (Tracy, 2003, 36–37).

THE CHALLENGES OF VALUES

Values are often so deeply imbedded in the culture that people have trouble articulating them. Challenges to the development of new statements of values include the following:

"It goes without saying." Before populating Web sites, thoughts on values very often lived only in the realm of "it goes without saying." Most of the reasons for an institution's existence and those "special" ideas that make it different than surrounding institutions are "obvious" (Eckel and Kezar, 2003, 129). Care for the individual and love of learning are second nature. It is also obvious that these are not the core values of Verizon or Ford Motor Company. Nevertheless, not all universities feel the same way about even these simple values.

Remember Bill Cosby's parody of his son's graduation from a major New York institution? Roughly, it was: "Stand up. Sit down. You're graduated." Compare this with the individual care shown to graduates of small colleges. Which seems to hold "care for the individual" more deeply as a value? If this is truly a value, it must be evidenced in our decisions. Naming the graduate and listing his or her accomplishments is evidence. The decision on how to conduct graduation was made within the constraints of the value.

While basic education values can be easily referenced, the values that designate an institution as a unique place to work, study, and live are harder to enunciate. As classes of institutions, women's colleges, tribal colleges, historically black colleges and universities, and community colleges have carefully developed rationales for existence. Going beyond these "themes of class" becomes more challenging. Are not-for-profits really less cutthroat than for-profits? What does "less cutthroat" really mean?

An excellent example of "talk about values" comes from the debate over the meaning of affirmative action and diversity. One only need read articles written 20 years ago to realize how much more sophisticated the debate has become. Although some still represent the debate as two-sided, it now has many dimensions. Are those in the majority more benefited by diversity than those in the minority? What does it mean to lead a diverse life?

Other areas are only emerging. Can we value accountability? What is it about being part of this local community that we value? Does our value for our graduates equal our value for our dropouts? What part of our decisions is spiritual? Do we value our students enough to take some responsibility for our feeder institutions? Do our faculty and staff meetings reflect the values we wish to instill in our students? Do we engage our adjunct professors and part-time staffers in discussions about our values? What "mark" will our graduates carry with them?

Culture. Values are a major part of institutional culture (Eckel and Kezar, 2003, 28). They describe what is important and how one is supposed to do something. Values in the culture are knit together in a form that borders on legend. Unfortunately, we have come to view culture as "that negative thing that has to be changed before we can get anything done." It is true that some of the values in the cultural matrix prevent change, but not all. In most cases, like the values discussed above, even the change-blocking values are never mentioned.

Institutions may say they value individuals, but Bill Cosby's major university graduation showed a stronger value for celebrating the achievements of the institution than the graduates. Other values you will not find on the Web are the personal desire to be accepted, values for keeping the well-trodden path clear, and values to get along with others. This part of the culture makes change difficult. The strategic question then becomes, "How do we move toward our goals and still get along?" Getting along is valued, and anyone who wants to say, "The old cycle isn't working," will find that he or she is not getting along as well as before.

If caring for the individual is one of the values of the culture, then the ceremonies and legends of the college should showcase individual care and be made of stories about caring. Today's college legends are the sketches in the brochures and viewbooks that connect the college to the reader. They say, "Here is a story about a person just like you who was transformed because of this instance of our individual care." Not a great Greek myth, but a small, true-life story.

The culture the change makers want to shift is contained in the assembly of values of the university. The first step in shifting the values is acknowledging and naming as many values as possible, then highlighting those that may work against change. Values in conflict should also be highlighted. People are not likely to change their values, but they may accept solutions that demonstrate an awareness of and an accommodation for those values. Values in conflict can also be used to inform new solutions by taking from the strengths of each. Thus, values clarification as begun by many institutions and evidenced on their Web pages is an integral part of the strategic process. For the same reason consultants proclaim that the culture must be shifted before change can happen, the code of silence needs to be stripped away from institutional values. Strategic change requires that values be used as part of the code of conduct of the institution. Human dignity requires that values be honored as part of the strategic process.

Why people say they work here. An excellent way to begin understanding institutional values is to open up a Web stream with the question: "Why do you work here instead of somewhere else?" Disregard (unless dominant) answers about "putting bread on the table" and "nowhere else would hire me." Look for threads of feeling that make the university unique. Look for the ways people are treated and what makes people feel good about working for the university. Look for the rewards people mention, bestowed by students and members of the community.

Why people work here is a strategic advantage. If a few people say that their best reward for working here came when one student said, "Thank you," then perhaps a small effort should begin to get students to think about thanking people a little more often. Does the university value individual humility and a willingness to share the personal credit for success? Is this sufficiently a part of the university's ethos to make it distinctive from other organizations? Taking this further, do efforts at the institution, from budgeting to team sports, demonstrate a "thank you" culture? Are e-mails always acknowledged to demonstrate that the person is thankful for the contact (and that the technology worked)? Are the teams acknowledged that are necessary to get work done? Are the same faces always in the alumni magazine, or is there a sense that everyone has become a part of the successes?

This is a narrow example and there are many other values that can be used to give a university distinction and to frame "how things ought to be done." The lesson, however, is to start with what exists: to start with those things that people already do and believe in. Let the community put words to it. Build on those words. Bossidy and Charan (2002, 89) call it "operationalizing culture."

SAMPLE VALUES

There are a basic number of broad values that can provide a foundation for institutional legend and that also are too broad to allow a university to differentiate itself, but that can be elaborated into more distinctive characteristic values. As broad areas, each value is more of a "what we do" rather than "how we do it" nature. The search for how *we* do it leads to distinction and strategic advantage (Birnbaum, 1988, 75).

The value of learning. This value is a fundamental tenant of educational institutions. To some degree all educational institutions value learning and growth by students, faculty, staff, administrators, and the organization as a whole. Like most of the great concepts, learning is hard to define well. In fact, as soon as we develop a measurable, common definition, we limit the concept. When we have a standardized test of "aptitude," we devalue the emotional growth that many colleges foster so well.

Distinctions among institutions come from the degree of responsibility taken for learning and growth and by the breadth of the responsibility. The Western Association of Schools and Colleges requests that institutions demonstrate a "culture of assessment" in self-studies performed for an accreditation review. Evidence of student learning has become the fundamental basis of this demonstration. Some institutions, just beginning to take this responsibility seriously, offer crude samples, like a scattering of test scores and faculty impressions. Other institutions present full portfolios of student work and development, demonstrating development over many dimensions.

Some institutions have a new focus on undergraduate education. Exemplifying a broader perspective, one community college's value-laden vision statement seemed to put nearly equal weight on student learning, community support, and staff development. This college took the value for student learning and said, "Hey, this applies to all of us, even the staff."

Value of social mobility. Many institutions pride themselves on the number of "first-generation college" students they enroll. These institutions are clearly engines of social mobility. Few institutions, however, quantify this value. Social mobility is generally thought of as class mobility, where class is measured by income level. Turning out graduating classes whose parents didn't have as high a proportion of college degrees is fairly good evidence of social mobility. Nevertheless, there are less-measurable elements of class with cultural and academic attributes that needed to be added to the assessment.

The two parts of social mobility are input and throughput. Does the institution serve a large proportion of students who have the potential for upward social movement? Does the institution succeed in graduating these students? Holding to this value requires that the institution track the socioeconomic status of incoming students. An upward drift would indicate that other values have started replacing this value. Graduation rates become key indicators that the existing support systems are succeeding with this group of students.

In the 1970s I was associated with an institution that prided itself on the excellence of its incoming students. The student newspaper liked to parody the institution for its success with downward social mobility. The counterculture tendencies of the scions of wealthy parents made for predictions of an impoverished life after graduation, far down the social ladder from parents. Although this was an ephemeral phenomenon, it does demonstrate that not all institutions do, nor should, value (upward) social mobility similarly.

Value of breaking down barriers and breaking through boundaries. Institutions that value access demonstrate a concern that the barriers between people and learning and the boundaries that surround the institution be broken. Although low socioeconomic status is usually indicative of a barrier and the two values often seem to overlap, careful analysis will differentiate the two. Institutional success with social mobility can simply mean successfully moving students who come from lower status backgrounds through to degrees, even though they may face no barriers. It is now possible to select students from families where degrees are rarely found who have great potential and few barriers.

An emphasis on breaking down barriers focuses on students who face difficulties entering college and then succeeding to graduation. Barriers include financial limitations, problems with preparation, prejudice, and family beliefs. A bad attitude toward education can also be substantial barrier, but few institutions have consciously tried to lower this barrier.

City College in New York is a shining example of an institution that became dedicated to breaking down financial and prejudice barriers by being nearly costless (alumni talk of only needing to raise the nickel for subway fare to get to classes) and by being open to Jews long before the middle of the 20th century. This was at a time when the Ivies had rigid quotas for the religious minority, allowing City to graduate a fair number of eventual Nobel Prize winners.

Many of today's institutions have successfully lowered the barriers of finance and prejudice with low tuitions, high scholarships, and affirmative action in admitting less represented groups. High tuition alone represents a barrier to many students from families with no experience in higher education, knowing little about scholarship possibilities.

A value aimed at helping students barred by poor preparation can be very appropriate for colleges serving areas with failing secondary schools, but it can also be very challenging. Like the social mobility value, this value has two aspects: access and success. The number of students admitted with whom the institution is taking a chance can measure access. Success is the proportion of these students that gain a degree (excluding transfers, unless data can also be gathered that shows the proportion of students who transfer and subsequently gain a degree). A quantitative approach to this value can clarify the institutional tactic for breaking down barriers. What proportion of new students is the institution willing to take a chance on? What is the minimum level of success (measured by graduation rate) for these students before the institution declares it has failed in its ability to support these students through to success? Few governmental entities are willing to support a program with a 75 percent failure rate, yet the institution may fully value and strongly support a program where 25 percent of the students who were doomed to a life of failure are moved through to success.

Competitive advantage is possible by articulating the value in terms that define action. Without analyzing the value of breaking down barriers, legislatures will come to see only irresponsibility in the vagueness of the claim. Incorporating the value of breaking down barriers means assessing it within a strategic framework. A value of breaking down barriers must acknowledge a value for financial responsibility. The strategic application of the value is never "We will admit tons of students who have little chance of succeeding and watch them fail." The strategic application should be "We will admit all students for whom we have the resources to give a reasonable chance of success." Then the institution must define terms.

Value of knowledge creation. The creation and dissemination of knowledge is a fundamental value of many universities. Differentiation comes in many forms: the degree of institutional support, the quality of physical facilities, the engagement of undergraduates in research projects, and the rate of production of commercially accepted ideas.

Value of civility. I have always been amazed by the variation in the ethos of civility from university to university with even greater variation from department to department. I can offer little wisdom in this area other than, if your institution appears to value civility, celebrate it.

There are many pieces to civility. Language can seem innocent, but certain words may be a torturer's tool, even in an innocent context. "I didn't say that you were railroading." "What do you mean, 'railroading'!" Intent is nothing. Perception is everything. A personal attack is just bait. Don't rise to it. Only ideas, plans, and theories are worthy of examination, not motivation or background.

Value of giving to the community. While this is discussed as a strategic component below, in some institutions the intention of being strongly imbedded in the community is held as a value. That is, it is not only a strategic key to the future, it is also a way of acting that always takes into account the health of the surrounding neighborhoods. The attitude extends beyond consideration of the effect of a decision on the community to actively designing programs for the betterment of the community. Some institutions are islands in their communities. Others are seen as expressions of the community. Members of island campus communities do not express this value strongly.

Value of involvement. How "cool" is it for students to be involved in community work? How cool is it for faculty members to spend "quality time" with students? Are administrators seen with students outside of the safety of their offices? This is an example of a value that seems to change over time. Although leadership has some effect, the winds that push involvement toward "cool" are not well determined or easily predictable. Involvement may be slightly more likely to be valued at community colleges. Religious institutions seem to find involvement an extension of their faith.

Value of financial independence. How strongly does the institution value freedom from regulation? The most extreme example is Hillsdale College, whose refusal to allow government-subsidized funding for students has exempted it from numerous federal regulations. Public universities are trading decreased state funding for greater decisionmaking independence. Religious colleges are finding themselves at odds with their founding religious boards and are occasionally pulling away.

Value of ceremony. Some colleges really know how to do a good ceremony. The value for ceremony is expressed by high participation and attention to the details within the ceremony. In many senses, the expression of value for ceremony signals higher attention to the values of the organization in general.

Ceremonies are used within cultures to clarify and transmit values. They can be initiation rites (orientations, faculty teas, convocations) and last rites (commencements, graduations). They can be annual celebrations (staff picnics, holiday parties) or one-time-only celebrations (project-end parties, inaugurations).

Successful transmission of values is not measured in the quality of the speeches but in the involvement of the participants in the expression of values. The raucous cheer for an individual graduate from family and friends is more meaningful than a hundred "Go forth!" exhortations from honored speakers. The president whose inauguration consisted of leading a team to build a house for Habitat for Humanity proclaimed more about institutional values than the usual pomp of red-, purple-, and black-caped and capped visitors.

Value of risk taking and being wrong. Few institutions value risk taking. Those that do make it clear what kinds of risks can be taken and what level of risk is tolerable. Sanctions are not imposed for bad outcomes, only improperly re-searched and presented risks. That is, in these institutions the sins are in not taking a risk, in not evaluating the degree of risk, and in doing a poor job of presenting the level of risk to the campus community.

Value of common sense. As institutions become more and more policy and plan bound, fewer members of the community feel free to make decisions that are simply expressions of common sense. In some institutions common sense is an adequate defense of any decision and failure to use common sense is a firing offense.

Even if a university has a rule that no current or former student who is in-debted to the university may be given an official transcript, a student who cannot pay the debt without a job and cannot get a particular job without a transcript should be given one. It's common sense.

Values are a necessary part of strategic thinking. Values are used in day-to-day decisionmaking to set constraints on the ways that decision implementation may be conducted. Values are also strategic because they are an important differentia-tor of universities (Eckel and Kezar, 2003, 129). The way one does things should be distinctive. Distinction is one way to approach market advantage.

A Day in the Life: Father David Pearson, CFO, Wyoming Loyola College

Father Pearson was at his computer this morning. He could see the low range of hills that obscured the continental divide from his window. The day was cool and dry this second day of November. He had decided to spend a few moments engaging the streaming discussion of institutional values that had been edited by the campus chaplain. While he felt that the discussion on the value of service had been very moving and sophisticated in the Jesuit tradition, he also felt that some part of the college's distinction, given this region, had not been covered. He confronted the "cowboy individualism" among his staff members and the students he met nearly every day. He knew, however, that the college founders strongly valued collective responsibility and the sense of self that comes with belonging.

He had worked hard to build a team spirit among staff members in the business office. He had found much resistance from among the Wyoming natives, contrasted with the ease with which the handful of staffers from immigrant families, especially those from the Hmong ranchers, participated in project teams. In his visits to other institutions in the area, he always found the spirit of individualism quite alive, almost celebrated, and a major block to any collective effort.

At WLC the religious found collective action to be natural and an enormously important part of their lives. Now, facing his computer screen, he wanted to make this value a more conscious expression of something that all members of the campus community would take with them when they left. He also wanted a forum where the project teams he had put together would more carefully explore the difficulties they faced when working as a team.

He typed, "I would like to open up a new stream that explores the value of collective thought." He then erased "collective thought" and tried, "teamwork." "This isn't going to be easy," he thought. He knew that he did not want to denigrate individualism. He just wanted to show that the college's spirit valued the development of skills for working together and that this was a sort of hallmark of the success of the college.

"Perhaps I had better start over after I talk to Father Smith after services. This dialogue is his. He should have ideas about how I can phrase my opening," thought Father Pearson. He then backed out of the dialogue without transmission and picked up the phone.

Seven Key Thoughts

1. When the end is the sole justification for the means, values have been neglected. Values are statements about *how* things are done. Values proclaim that there are proper ways of doing things not determined by the result.

2. Values are strategic because they define proper ways of implementation and because they are an important part of differentiation. Values clarification and expression is an important phase of the process of strategic thinking, because the process allows continual exploration of nongoal guidance. While goals allow differentiation and competitive success, so does differentiation of means.

3. Values often exist without clarification or even expression. Values can become so taken for granted that they can be forgotten. New members fail to heed the guidance. External groups fail to perceive the special qualities.

4. A higher education institution values education, but not all universities express the value in the same way. Who is covered (just students or all members of the campus community)? Is education just intellectual development, or does it encompass emotional, social, and spiritual development?

5. Universities also differ on where they fall on the continuum from value free to value-laden. Some institutions are much more prescriptive as to "how things are done." Others value the free expression of individual values very highly. Deciding where the university falls on this continuum is strategic. One end, however, is not necessarily more strategic than the other.

6. Values form the superstructure of institutional culture. The tenants of culture are institutional values.

7. Key values are imbedded in the history and origin of the institution and are slow to change. Even institutions that move away from the control of founding groups tend to retain most of the founding values.

Chapter Eight

USING CONCEPTS AS A BRIDGE TO STRATEGIC THINKING

A major premise of strategic thought is that the university's ability to be successful can be jump-started with goals and a vision but cannot be sustained unless all members of the organization enroll in a process of acquiring greater understanding of inner university and surrounding systems. With the explication of each concept, universities have been able to move from a lower level of debate to a higher plane. And with greater concept clarity, universities have been able to fashion more precise strategies for change (Eckel and Kezar, 2003, 50). For example, a better understanding of the rules that must guide endowment payout has meant that the strategic focus can be moved from questions of, "Why can't we just spend it all now?" to "What financial policies will help us provide the same or better levels of service in the future as now?"

The goal for this chapter is to grasp how institution-wide intellectual control of particular concepts has improved strategic thought.

SAMPLE CONCEPTS

Financial equilibrium. This concept came out of the work of David Hopkins and William Massy (1981, 39–40) in the 1970s at Stanford. They were looking for an idea that would serve as a regulatory guide for the university financial models they were developing. Financial equilibrium exists if a set of financial policies causes the university to neither gain nor lose the functionality of assets. The financial policies of concern include guidance on rates of faculty pay increase, future tuition increase limitations, endowment payout rules, enrollment policies, scholarship awarding rules, and new academic program support rates. Assets include the quality of the faculty and staff, the vitality of the academic and research programs, the endowment, the physical plant, and net assets. (See Porter, 1992, 95, for an explanation of the necessity of defining assets more broadly.) In other words, a set of policies that could keep salaries competitive, maintain the support of the endowment, and balance the budget but could not stem the increase in deferred plant maintenance over a predicted 10-year period would be defined as out of financial equilibrium.

The concept of financial equilibrium brought each year's budget process into the context of long-term goals. The concept allowed budget discussions to move from parochial concerns about "my budget, this year" to strategic concerns about whether the tuition increase was part of a long-term approach or an aberration, and hence, a failure to adhere to strategies. Concerns went from whether the budget was balanced to whether the efforts to balance the budget could be sustained in any sort of policy framework without eroding the assets of the institution.

This concept pushed debate to focus on appropriate long-term strategies, instead of just this year's tuition or salary increase. Longer-term concerns entered the budget debate arena: "Is the strategic guide of keeping the tuition increase under family income increases sustainable? (See Warner [1992, 91].) Does the pressure on family income force families to increase the number of workers? Should the policy use stated tuition or tuition net of scholarships?" This concept allows a university the possibility of breaking the "announce, protest, implement" cycle. At least new stages are added for discussion of the policy and for protest that the new tuition does not follow the policy.

Intergenerational equity. Hopkins and Massy (1981, 67) also used this concept in the 1970s. This concept provides a rational benchmark for endowment payout rules. Financial equilibrium is partially derivative of this concept in that it too declares that future generations should enjoy the same level of college services that current students enjoy.

Intergenerational equity is preserved if payout policies neither penalize nor favor future generations in terms of the purchasing power of the endowment over extended time. If the policies would allow spending from the endowment, including gains, losses, and earnings, of $10 million, then those same policies, consistently applied, would result in a spending amount in any future year *that could buy the same items as the $10 million bought today.* The benefit of the endowment to future generations remains the same.

The choice of benchmark then becomes challenging. If endowment payout is used to purchase roughly the same things as are bought under the general budget, then the university should use a benchmark of a forecast of inflation for a mixture of salaries and other purchases in the same proportion as is done under the budget. If endowment payout is largely used for scholarships, then the appropriate benchmark is projected tuition growth. Mixtures of the two would call for a proportionate average of the two benchmarks.

The promise of equity among generations, however, is hedged with a warning that it only works as well as the inflation, appreciation, gift levels, and earnings predictions work. Equity exists only as intent, not as outcome. Outcome may require revision of the forecasts.

The concept can be made more sophisticated by building in buffers to ease the impact of short-term fluctuations. Various payout-smoothing rules are introduced. Any costs of these buffers must be factored in and equity preserved in the long run, including these costs.

The concept brings new strategic questions. Should the rate of gifts to endowment be included as an offset to spending? That is, should new gifts be considered additions to the responsibility of support of the endowment, or part of the endowment's increased ability to support? With the former, the payout rate is depressed to preserve the spending power of the existing corpus. With the later, the payout rate can be higher, because gifts are considered as "refueling."

If the gifts are restricted to a new purpose, it seems clear they are not contributing anything to the support of existing programs. Thus, policies seeking to provide equal support for future generations should not factor in the rate of restricted gift support. Unrestricted gifts to endowment pose a more difficult question. Should they be considered available to support existing programs and factored into the equity equation? Should they be considered additional support, where the giver is seeking additional advantage for future generations? Or, should only a portion of predicted unrestricted gift additions to endowment be used in the equity calculation? Clearly these are strategic questions that can greatly affect current and future financial fortunes. Had Stanford excluded the gifts to endowment assumption (an addition equal to 2 percent of the value of the endowment was assumed to be coming in through gifts each year), the payout rate would have to have been lowered by two percentage points during the 1970s. This would have had an enormous budget impact in those years, but endowment would have grown considerably larger, reflecting the wish that new gifts support new things. Without the concept, these strategic concerns could not have been pursued.

Complexity. Institutions are most aware of the impact of increasing complexity through the growing imposition of government regulations. The impact of growing complexity is also found in each year's new administrative computing software, the technology demands of programs, the sophistication of viruses transmitted over the Internet, and the range of student abilities and student learning requirements.

Awareness of changing levels of complexity is the first step in managing it. Institutions take very seriously each new set of government regulations on financial aid, reporting, international students, and privacy. Institutions are also getting better at estimating the costs of these increases to complexity. The estimates from major universities of hundreds of thousands of dollars to implement new government rules on tracking international students appear to be carefully developed.

A more limited view is evident when universities evaluate new technologies. No standard for rating complexity exists. Fortunately, few universities are surprised these days when newly implemented technology saves no money. Usually a few core processes become much more efficient, but managing the processes requires more skill (and pay) and newly added capabilities also require managing. In the end, the little efficiency gained is spent on managing new and more sophisticated processes.

Growing complexity is also seen in the curriculum. More and more must be learned before graduation. Preparing a gentleman for governing just isn't what it used to be.

As we learn more about the challenges of complexity, we realize the strategic importance of dealing with its seemingly unstoppable growth. Academic, financial, and service strategies that do not address the growing range of needs seem naïve. We do not often know where or when the next new bit of complexity is going to appear, but we certainly know that it will.

Learning. The old metaphor of pouring the wine of wisdom into an empty vessel seems to be drifting away. The degree of independence of learning from teaching is better understood. Still, we know very little about learning. We try various new techniques and then test, but the tests are very limited measures of learning. From those studies we have begun to realize how little we know (Travers, 1972, 2–5).

Because we know so little about learning, we have only begun to realize the tremendous differences among people in learning methods. Take as an example the differences among people in the use of mental images in learning. Unfortunately, there seems to be no one level of ability to hold mental images. Some people see perfect images in three dimensions and can easily manipulate these images. Others have never seen a mental image. Both can learn, but clearly the learning strategies must be different. We have usually assumed much uniformity in learning when we have designed our instruction. At best we have differentiated between "fast and slow." With the latest work in cognitive psychology, we are coming to the point where we often tell students to do "what works for them."

How relevant can our academic strategies be without better understanding of learning?

Accountability. By mandate, we are to become more accountable (Green, 1988b, 35; Balderston, 1995, 8). We are finding, however, that what "accountable" means to the legislature is not necessarily what we thought it meant. The meaning of "accountable" seems to be shifting from being able to accurately report and justify all expenditures to being able to demonstrate that core processes are effective: students are learning, and knowledge is being generated.

In strict terms accountability to someone has always meant getting agreement with that person on responsibilities and demonstrating to that person's satisfaction that the responsibilities have been met. "Getting agreement" is the problem. Whereas institutions eagerly took responsibility for inputs, like numbers of freshmen and their test scores, and for outputs, like numbers of graduates, universities are now being asked to be accountable for transformations. What have the students learned? Even the output standards have shifted from counts to quality: "They don't even know that John Quincy Adams was the sixth president—a simple, basic fact!"

Accountability's impact on strategic direction awaits its greater explication as a concept. It is clear that until universities work with their constituencies to come to a greater understanding of what is meant by "accountable," the constituencies will feel that promises are being broken. A university that can say, "This is what we are accountable for" and that can get at least a nod from several constituencies will then need to build strategies that push in that direction.

Assessment. Assessment has a more private connotation than accountability does. Assessment as a concept, however, does cover all phases of institutional work life. Comfort with the concept of assessment means that each decision and endeavor can and should be evaluated at various points, including points long after implementation. Assessment means that we fold into every process an early stage where we ask, "When and how will we know we have been successful?" We will ask at an intermediate stage, "Do we think we will be successful?" and "Has our definition of success changed?" We will also ask at the end, "What might we have done differently?" "What will we do differently next time?" and "Did we achieve some things that we did not expect?" We build assessment into big projects, like system implementations, and everyday, ongoing work, like registration events.

This feeble outline of the concept serves to illustrate how much we all could learn about assessment. As members of an organization develop the concept, the implications for strategic direction become clearer. Strategies that call for pricing to bring in a particular group of students in greater numbers, with no assessment phase, will be viewed as hollow. How will we know that the strategy worked? How will we be able to demonstrate that our pricing strategy was effective or was some other factor of greater impact?

Imagine this: you are assigned to present to the trustees your university's strategic use of assessment. Where would you begin? What is the university's understanding of the meaning of assessment? Could you say that assessment is well understood by everyone and that it can be found as a part of all endeavors?

Randomness. Our faith in the value of statistical tests rests on an understanding of a rather difficult concept: randomness. True randomness is equivalent to "uncaused" behavior. Our understanding of the concept, however, is that something causes random behavior, but we just don't know what it is. We use the concept strategically when we say we will be the agent of achieving some goal. We proclaim that we shall be the cause of the change. If the change happens, we take credit. We, however, often fail to understand the complexity of human-based systems. The complexity obscures all the tiny elements of causality, and when replication fails, we are confused. We thought that we had an impact.

Our descriptions of the results of human action are often nothing more than arithmetic means. Actual behavior usually fails to hit the mean, deviating in one or the other direction (should there only be two dimensions). We may intend that an increased advertising budget will bring in more freshmen, but do we really have any idea of all the factors that influence a potential student's decision? There may be an increase this time but not next.

Understanding random behavior and the slow progression from uncaused to caused helps move strategic thinking more toward realistic ideas, goals, and directions. Human actions are like the actions of molecules of air: the motion appears random, Brownian movement, related to temperature, but each change in direction is caused by a bump, and our attempts to measure any single molecule changes its momentum. Our quest is to predict the bump, yet the more we know about behavior, the greater our challenge seems.

The search for adequate conceptual models to inform decisionmaking continues. (See Knerr [1990].) How we understand and how we think about a system influences our choice of strategies, and it influences the decisions we make.

A Day in the Life: Jerry Pilgrim, Professor of Philosophy, Brendom University

"Hey, Jerry. How's the 'Concept Czar' today?" came the call from behind the professor as he walked down the hall of the arts building at Brendom.

It was A. Z. Thompkins, CFO at Brendom. "Hey, A. Z.! How are you?" Jerry replied.

"Feeling good. Feeling like giving you a little trouble on your new job with the strategy team," A. Z. grinned at Jerry. They were old friends and tennis partners. The CFO was rarely in the arts building, so Jerry found his presence a little surprising.

"What brings you over here?" Jerry questioned A. Z.

"Fire inspectors coming next week. I thought I would yell at the pottery people *before* the inspectors came instead of *after*," A. Z. explained. "I also wanted to tell you that I thought the piece we did on financial equilibrium came out quite well in the online strategy newsletter. What are you working on now?"

"Yup! Bill Presley in Math told me he learned a lot from the article but still couldn't ride his unicycle. Uh . . . that's a joke, I guess. Anyway, I'm now working on the concept: judgment."

"Great! I'll take two." It didn't seem that either was ready to stop joking. "OK, What do you mean?" A. Z. tried to get serious.

"Well, our strategic directions are supposed to influence our everyday decision, right?" said Jerry.

"Yes," A. Z drawled.

"And an important piece of every decision is judgment, right?"

"Right."

"Then how come we don't know much about it?" questioned Jerry.

"Hey, I know it when I see it," replied A. Z.

"Perfect. That is, concepts that we only 'know when we see them' are the best candidates for further explication, especially when we know they are somehow related to driving this truck called a university."

"Okay. Judgment is when somebody guesses right," A. Z. pronounced.

"Nope. Guess again," Jerry fed back. "That is, judgment has more to do with putting together all the factors involved in a decision and being alert to the decision situation than it has to do with being lucky about the final decision."

"Okay, but 'factors involved in a decision' is pretty vague. Do you have something more to go on?" asked A. Z.

"No, but that's what's going to make this more interesting than just you and me sitting down and wording something on equilibrium. I'm going to put this up on the strategy Web page as a question and get an open dialog going. Of course, I will do a little private lobbying with my fellow philosophy dudes to boost participation. But I think that getting people to talk about the meaning of judgment to them will put a little more meat on the concept."

"Okay, I get it," said A. Z. "But now I've got some kilns to fire, so to speak."

"No problem. Are we still on for 5:30 Thursday at the West Courts?"

"That's the racquet." A. Z. turned and headed for the studio wing, while Jerry tried to remember where he had been going.

Seven Key Thoughts

1. Deliberate attention to conceptual development runs parallel to all the levels of strategic thought. A changing, more sophisticated grasp of a good concept can be a driving force to strategic development.

2. Conceptual understanding of the workings of internal systems improves the accuracy of policy decisions. Taking the mystery out of things like endowments and learning through distance education is necessary to engage the university community in a realistic strategic debate.

3. Conceptual understanding of environmental systems improves anticipation of change. Likewise, taking some of the mystery out of things like legislative judgments and insurance premiums can raise the level of discussion.

4. Concepts that people seem to know intuitively may be good candidates for exploration. Judgment, learning, teaching, and research are things we seem to avoid delving very deeply into. We ought to try to know a little more about these fundamental pieces of core university processes, however.

5. Once a concept seems to be really understood and used, it is time to examine it all over again. There is no better way to understand the limitations of a concept than to try to apply it.

6. Concepts grow creaky with age, not because they are wrong or irrelevant, but because our growing sophistication makes them simplistic. The question becomes: What more do we wish to know?

7. A good concept is like a great painting: every time you look at it, you see something new. A good concept has a richness that brings some amount of shared meaning to each person, while giving new insights to all.

Chapter Nine
PRINCIPLES—THE LYNCHPIN OF STRATEGIC THOUGHT

The use of principles within strategic planning, as examined in this chapter, are the lynchpins of strategic thought, connecting the goals of the vision to the present by way of strategies within value guidance. Principles are the rally flags around which constituents can gather, even when specific choices of action are contested.

Because of their rigorous structure, principles can be developed for many endeavors. They can make strategic thinking more rigorous; they can make a meeting go more smoothly. They should be enunciated at the top of every meeting agenda to explain the purpose of the meeting. They should be developed for any project plan to present the purpose of the project. They may even be used in curriculum development to focus the planning group on outcomes and style.

Because principles can be fairly abstract, members of any group can more easily agree on them than they can on specific actions. Agreement on principles is a necessary first step before hammering out action plans, especially those that may require compromise. Principles give a common ground and a litmus test to action ideas. Kouzes and Posner (2002, 45) are firm about how matters of principle, based on values, are required of leaders. In any organization where people outside of the center are making critical decisions daily, strategic principles are a guide (Gadiesh and Gilbert, 2001, 154).

Structure. Principles begin with a goal statement derived from the vision, often with a subsection of quantitative specifications. The next section mentions the strategy that will be used to achieve the goal. The final section discusses values to be used. It is a style section that talks about how the group will conduct itself in achieving the goals. The resulting principle is often a single, clumsy sentence that packs in too much, or three or four well-connected sentences. These are carefully constructed guides, not marketing slogans. The sections are:

1. Visionary goal statement, indicating purpose
    a. General specification (the "we will . . ." section)
    b. Any measurable specifics that indicate goal achievement (the "such that/as a result . . ." section)

2. Chosen strategy indication (the "by doing/undertaking/attempting/ following/ implementing . . ." section)
3. Values or style specification (the "in a way that . . ." section)

For example, Freding University has a vision of becoming a model of service to high-risk students. University leaders have agreed on a strategy and have already settled on the strategic risk level. They do not know what programs they will use to do this, but after much discussion, they believe they can agree on this principle. This example uses a high degree of quantitative goal specificity.

Freding University **will** become a national model of success with students having a broad range of academic preparation, **such that** the 15 percent of each entering class that will be high-risk students (SAT scores below 850) will graduate at a rate 20 percentage points above the rate established by the 1995 cohort after six years by 2005 **by implementing** the "Every Student is a Special Program Student" strategy, **in a way that** focuses on the basic human dignity of every student.

Another example at a completely different level would be a principle (one of several, possibly) heading a meeting agenda for a strategy development group.

In the first 45 minutes of the meeting The Strategy Development Team **will** develop strategic ideas for increasing retention from the freshman to sophomore year, **such that** we will end with a list of 50 **by using** brainstorming techniques, **in a way that** no ideas will be criticized in any verbal or nonverbal manner.

Focus. Principles are primarily a means to bring focus to the strategic elements that are most important for achieving success. Requiring a list of more than six principles usually indicates that focus has been lost and the plan has become a list of projects. In the first example above, retention of high-risk students is a critical element in the strategic direction of the university. This particular example of a principle, however, may only be a principle for the retention improvement team. The university may have found that thinking in terms of overall retention, or even overall enrollment management, is the appropriate level.

For example, a higher-level principle might be: Catapult Community College **will** be a primary force in Catapult County's educational achievement goal, **such that** 35 percent of all county residents, regardless of income or ethnicity, hold at least an associates degree, **by using** improved primary and secondary education intervention and support strategies and **by using** the student as mentor retention strategy, **in a way that** increases participation in the direction of the college by residents, students, parents, and members of the primary and secondary school community.

This example is flawed in that the strategies are too specific. Such specific strategies should be a product of the principle-building process, not an input.

Construction. I have not found the development of principles to be particularly amenable to online processes. Real face-to-face meetings are needed to develop the intensity of focus necessary. The difficulty of getting just the right wording is extremely challenging. Also, the tendency to want to specify the projects can quickly derail both face-to-face and online work. Facilitators need to keep raising the level of abstraction to prevent members from drifting into side arguments over specific programs and from jumping on a project bandwagon, forgetting to specify what they wanted to achieve in the first place.

A meeting agenda designed to guide principle development might be:
1. What are the really big things we wish to achieve?
2. How will we know when we have done so?
3. For each one, what basic strategies should we pursue?
4. For each one, what will be our style for doing so?

There are good reasons for starting a strategic thought process with an attempt to construct principles. The discussion focuses ideas about vision, strategies, and values. The discussion moves people away from listing their favorite projects. The discussion can be revisited after online work on vision, strategies, and values has brought in a wider range of ideas from more sectors of the campus community.

Practice. Kouzes and Posner (2002, 47) suggest that organizational leaders spend a few moments each day asking themselves whether they have pursued any actions that demonstrate the values and principles they have proclaimed as critical. An important characteristic of leaders is the ability to move "above themselves" and examine their actions within the framework of the principles. In a quiet moment at the end of the day (and, one hopes, there are a few), a president or CFO should examine the day in terms of the principles he or she has laid out for the university. "Was I able to make the university more strategically competitive within this principle? What will I do tomorrow to make the university more strategically competitive within this principle?"

Because the components of principles are given much more attention in this book, the conceptual portion of this chapter is not long. The "Day in the Life" profile in this chapter may be more helpful in learning the use of principles in strategic thinking.

A Day in the Life: Jalal Hashemi,
President, Paul De Sain College

Dr. Hashemi was at his large oak desk putting the finishing touches on his "Six College Principles" early on a Saturday in the fall. At noon he was planning to greet the alumni gathered for an "event" lunch before the big soccer game with PDSC's archrival, Bigginton College. He decided to read the draft out loud to see if it had any sonority at all. It was perhaps too early in the drafting stage, but . . .

"Paul De Sain College will be the premier private college producer in the three-state region of thoughtful citizens and productive leaders in civic, business, and the not-for-profit sector. This will be measured by graduate and alumni organizational responsibility levels, in a way that demonstrates PDSC's values of service to the community. As a result, Paul De Sain College will be the primary choice in the three-state region among college-bound seniors in one-to-one application/acceptance rate comparisons against all regional, high-quality private colleges.

"Paul De Sain College will produce leaders committed to their communities, as demonstrated by in-school and alumni participation in community or volunteer activities, in a way that reaches out to students at all levels of academic preparation. The result will be that all individuals committed to change will be drawn to the college.

"Paul De Sain College will nurture the spiritual, intellectual, emotional, and physical potential of every member of its community in a way that, perhaps, neglects the material portion of the world. The result will be that the bond between students, alumni, faculty, and staff remains strong for the life of each individual.

"Paul De Sain College will begin an integration of its programs, emphasizing the continual learning within the liberal arts with technical skill building in specific areas, in a way that fosters systemic, computational, environmental, leadership, and social literacy within every program of study. The result will be that every PDSC graduate is comfortable with the complexities, responsibilities, and continual learning necessary in the lives of successful and responsible people.

"Paul De Sain College will take responsibility for the success of every matriculated student, in a way that demonstrates that the learner is the center of the PDSC universe. The result will be that even students who transfer elsewhere or are unable to remain in college may say that they gained by the experience of matriculating at Paul De Sain College.

"Paul De Sain College will take responsibility for the growth of all faculty and staff members in a way that evidences the philosophy of community service and concern of the founder, Paul De Sain. The result will be that promotion, increased responsibility, low turnover, and individual initiative are the watchwords of every member of the community."

"Either I have too few measurable goals in this, or the ones I have bring down my attempt at lofty language," he thought. "Perhaps the staff can help me with that issue. Those 'measurables' really are a drag on the language, but the consultant kept telling me I needed them. Maybe I can stick them in an appendix," he thought, with some sarcasm.

He then thought ahead to the doors that he would be closing with these "Principles." "There goes the MBA program proposal," he thought. "At least there goes the initial proposal. As 'vanilla' as it is, it just doesn't show the bias toward community service and the liberal arts that these principles affirm. Maybe it can be revived as an MPA, but then, MBA programs, especially new ones, aren't the guaranteed successes they once were. We probably need to develop something that is uniquely 'Paul De Sain.'"

He also thought about the stumbling effort to raise funds for a new student union. With some relief he thought that these principles might kill that. The principles justify avoiding the sale of creature comforts. Nevertheless, he realized the college was going to need to be very careful in evaluating its programs and environment in terms of "classiness," where "well-worn" could be a virtue as long as it was not "tawdry." He feared he might start a huge debate by trying to split hairs.

He knew that these principles would force him to bring the efforts of the assistant dean for volunteer activities to the fore. Perhaps they would justify a full dean's position, with much broader responsibilities.

He was feeling a touch of pride at the way he had elevated the freshman program by asking the college to find pride in its dropouts, when he heard a knock.

The soccer coach entered, "Hi Jerry," the coach said. "I thought you might like company on your way to the lunch."

The president always brightened at the sound of his American nickname. "That would be great. Just a second while I make a few copies, and I'll be right with you." He punched a few keys on the computer and the printer whirred to life as he pulled on his suit coat.

"Is the team already there?" he asked.

"Yes, the ladies are there, already charming the alumni into a team endowment. They wanted to wear their uniforms, but I required slacks," the coach grinned.

"And now, it is our duty to charm as well. Shall we go, Ma'am?" The president and the coach walked out into the crisp air of late fall.

Seven Key Thoughts

1. Principles are the action link between vision, strategies, and values. Principles are the sinews that tie critical levels of strategic thought together.

2. A principle begins with "We will . . ." (What is the vision that we are pursuing?), followed by "such that or as determined . . ." (How will we know that we have succeeded?), then followed by "by implementing . . ." ("What strategies shall we employ to approach our vision?), and finished with "in a way that . . ." (What values do we want to exhibit while achieving this?).

3. Compromises are more workable at the level of actions than at the level of beliefs, strategies, vision, and values. Agreement is easier to obtain at higher levels of abstraction, like beliefs and vision, because members of a university community share many of the same ideals. It is important to get agreement at this level, by developing principles carefully, before getting down to the arguments over implementation.

4. Structured principles provide focus at a high level of abstraction. By limiting the number of principles, the focus of the institution is automatically pointed toward the most critical factors for success.

5. By limiting the number of principles, the really important aspects of the vision are highlighted. Visions can become very detailed and can include many items that current trends will cause to happen without intervention. Principles can be used to show the ones that will require the most intervention.

6. Principles highlight values in action. Principles with an "in a way that . . ." section raise awareness of the importance of unique style that highlights the institution and the strategy. One of the keys of principle statements is to show how members of the university community are to conduct themselves while achieving this goal. This puts words to the idea that there are some things that cannot be well measured and that can only be demonstrated by how we do them.

7. In a similar manner, principles provide statements of the broad strategies that will be used to achieve the vision. What is omitted is also part of the communication.

Chapter Ten
STRATEGY DEVELOPMENT

In the rush to bring closure to a lengthy strategic planning process, universities tend to leap from mission, vision, and goals to projects without seeking ways to improve strategic thinking during each day. Universities that bypass strategic thought development have only a weak rational basis for their strategic projects. Martorana and Kuhns (1975, 162–63) suggest the importance of strategies for academic change. Pearson (1999, 48) reports on the "transformative" power of strategy itself. What follows is a description of the structure of strategies.

STRATEGIC THINKING

The basis of all strategic thought is the question, "How can we be successful at achieving our mission?" A strategy is a way of proceeding that leads toward mission success. Mission success is presented in the vision, a tangible picture of what the university will look like once it achieves its strategic goals. Be careful not to work backward from successful completion of projects to vision. "I see an institution with a fully functional, fifth-generation student information system" does not work as a vision element. The mission of the institution is not "To provide staffers with the latest tools to access student information." The mission needs to be something about providing learning, improving understanding, and building the civil competence of some audience that has such needs. The vision states the visible evidence for success. Perhaps, something like, "I see a university where the graduates are 20 percentage points more likely than other graduates to gain leadership positions in public agencies and public service organizations."

Not very sexy, but I don't recommend thinking these up alone. Devising appropriate vision ideas, mission statements, and strategies is not a deductive process. This book would be much easier to write, and probably unnecessary, if strategic development were not an inductive process.

The difference is easy to see. Deductive processes are those most amenable to the engineering and finance mind. We know what theory is correct. The trick is to implement it properly and drive it all the way home. Someone hands the deductive specialist a hammer, and he or she starts driving nails. The "how-to" cookbooks give us "the formula" and tell us the best way to implement it. Unfortunately, a cookbook is not necessarily going to give us, in our institution's particular situation, the best set of strategies. We could get lucky, of course.

An inductive situation is one where we do not know the proper theory to apply. The deductive approach to an inductive situation begins: 1. list all possible theories; 2. test all possible theories; and 3. implement the best one. In other words, list all possible strategies, and so forth. How do we know we have listed all possible strategies? How can we test even a few of them without getting diverted from what we are supposed to be doing? How can we be certain that any one is "best?" We clearly want to avoid a sedulously deductive approach to these very open-ended problems (Cyert and March, 1963, 291).

Observation tells us that two inductive methodologies are generally used. Either we can go with a hunch or we can build a process that keeps generating new strategic ideas, while developing better and better decision rules for choosing among them. I favor the latter. Nevertheless, the hunch method can work as well. Leaders can both be lucky and have amassed an enormous amount of experience and understanding to fuel their hunches. I certainly cannot prove that hunches don't work, but I can't write a book about how to do hunches either.

The more structured approach rests on these premises:

1. Because of the nature of an inductive process, a large range of possible ideas on possible strategies is the best way to begin.
2. The best way to get a large range of possible ideas is to tap the thoughts of many people.
3. Criticism of ideas at the early, idea-generating stage reduces the total number of ideas available. (See the brainstorming tips in Dolence, Rowley, and Lujan [1997, 10].)
4. A broader range of ideas can be generated if models and categories of strategies are given.

These premises suggest any number of group facilitation methods for generating ideas. Because this is an idea-generating, not an implementation, stage, large groups can be invited to participate (up to 50 in many situations), and several different groups can work on the same problems.

One popular facilitation technology has individuals write ideas on sticky notes and paste them in a sort of ceremony. Then there are generally several rounds of discussion to eliminate duplications and to add up concentrations, while reorganizing the ideas into coherent patterns. It is somewhat harder for the facilitator to impose a structure and teach a model for a proper strategy, but most are able to get the groups to fill in missing areas. It is much more difficult for facilitators to keep the groups at the strategic level. Many people just want to present their solution and let others name the strategy that would require it.

Kaplan and Norton (2001, 69–81) suggest strategic categories that fit a generic for-profit organization well. There are broad overlaps between these authors' "customer" strategy group and the "marketing" strategies discussed below. Similarly, their category, "internal," matches the categories of academics, research, and services below. (Also see Porter [1985, 11–25] for generic strategy structures.) The expanded categories below probably suit universities better. Generally, the strategy-generating groups need to be aware that there are overlapping strategies in marketing, academics, research, finance, community relationships, and services.

STRATEGIC CATEGORIES

Marketing Strategies

Marketing strategies are ideas on how potential students (and donors and legislators and parents and alumni . . .) will be reached with a message that builds loyalty (defined in terms of completion to degree, future support, positive word-of-mouth advertising, and legislative trust) to the university. Marketing strategies are based on an understanding of why people are trading resources for education (Tracy, 2003, 60). Marketing strategies are the methods the university uses to convey its value to the external world. This strategy is also used to guide other strategies in increasing that value.

Much of what goes on at a university must be connected to the overarching marketing strategy. This strategy attempts to change the way its many audiences perceive the university. This means that academic offerings, academic distinction, the cost of attendance, and the quality of services are all, in fact, part of the marketing strategy. Thus, academic strategies, research strategies, financial strategies, community relationship strategies, and service strategies all must be consistent with the marketing strategy. The marketing strategy, however, must be developed out of the mission.

A marketing strategy will have these elements:

1. **Visible areas of academic strength.** While this may not be the "real" reason a young person chooses a college, it is certainly a necessary one. The structure of a stated reason, especially when presented to adults, is "because it has a strong English program," or something similar. Because the mission is generally framed in terms of those who must be served, the academic strategy should work to make the available academic disciplines valuable to those groups. The academic strategy then becomes part of the marketing strategy. Thus, the marketing

strategy does not directly drive the academic strategy. Nevertheless, presenting value to those the institution serves is a straightforward marketing concern. Marketing, however, must work to make sure that the reality of academic strengths is part of the perceptions of the audiences.

Making the university's areas of academic strength more visible is thus the challenge of this facet of marketing strategies. Weaknesses in this strategy would be evident when administrative and faculty focus groups come up with far different answers from those of potential applicants and current students to questions like "What are the institution's academic strengths?" and "Why would you recommend that someone come to this university?"

The selection of this strategy requires that the university answer the fundamental question of, "What programs should it be offering that would be of value to its constituency?" and "How can it offer those programs in a way that would be of greater value than similar pro- grams offered by competitors?"

Changing this strategy, as a marketing strategy, however, requires ei- ther new strengths or changes to the perceptions of the constituency. Program specific marketing is used regularly for this purpose.

2. **Offering presentation.** Another common method of increasing the value of the university to its constituencies is by changing the presentation of the offering. Working adults like classes to meet in the evenings as few times per week as possible. Many institutions are finding that students with jobs and family responsibilities will take at least one course online in order to fit a reasonable load into a difficult schedule. These students say, "I do most of my work on this course after 9:00 p.m., when the kids are in bed." Weekend courses, online courses, and partially online courses have become very popular with nontraditional and even many traditional students.

    The flaw in many institutions' "distance learning strategies" comes from putting technology before the mission. Ask: "What audience are you planning to reach? How does that fit with your mission? If you are not serving these people now, how will they find out about you?

(Or, is this market at all concentrated?) Do you know with whom you are competing?" Technology must serve the mission. Technology is not an "answer" by itself. Distance learning is an "offering presentation" strategic tool, but to be strategic, it must fit within the overall set of strategies.

3. **Tangible student transformation strengths.** As mentioned above, potential students must weigh the potential transformation offered by each institution to some degree. Colleges and universities are, in general, offering to increase the probability of later personal success. They demonstrate this by pointing to the successes of graduates and with stories from current students and graduates that begin, "Yes, I was once just like you, but now..."

The transformations can take the form of job readiness, survival skills, self-confidence, increased and improved circle of friends, and general understanding. Interestingly, the transformation stories are strongest for those institutions that serve those with the furthest to go (Balderston, 1995, 287).

What is most troubling about our attitude toward this strategy is that we ignore 50 percent of our new students. That's the proportion that does not graduate in six years. Why aren't institutions more concerned about the impact they have on those that don't finish? We are taking a chance every time we admit a student. Why don't we work to improve the outcomes for those with whom we make a mistake?

This part of our marketing strategy is often underdeveloped. We hint at the transformation, but we rarely make a strong effort to improve the transformations we make. Too often we seek to emulate the wealthy universities, where transformation is of little importance. In those situations we try to avoid transformation by recruiting those who are already successful. Recruiting such students would be easier if our transformations were really successful.

4. **Known student comfort zones.** Institutions are known for drawing together like-minded students. Attracting students we know would never be happy or comfortable at our institution is a losing strategy for both the institution and the student. I worked at an institution

once that had no trouble drawing students away from more prestigious universities because it required that they have international experience. Students would tell me, "I could have gone to [a prestigious private university], but no one there would have known where Ouagadougou was. Here, everyone knows, and I've met other people who have been there." Obviously "comfort" is a wide term.

Comfort, in all its dimensions, is terribly important to students. Making sure that the dominant image of the institution does not exclude groups is also important. An institution made up only of football-rabid students is not desirable. The successes and lives of other types of students are included in marketing.

The marketing, however, is an offshoot of the more difficult part of the strategy: actually making the institution comfortable (but not too comfortable intellectually) for many types of students. The recent University of Michigan Supreme Court decision was based on the educational value of diversity to a certain extent. Nevertheless, many institutions are not comfortable places for all students.

Making the trade-off between the effectiveness of comfort and the effectiveness of diversity must be done explicitly with open dialogue among members of the campus community. Institutions will have to rob some of the value of diversity to improve comfort for others. The community has the right to determine when the institution might go too far in one direction or another.

5. **Palatable costs for students.** The main financial perception that affects institutional choice is economic burden. Older students sometimes think in terms of investments and the return of higher earnings, but this is rare. Very few these days just look at the sticker price and decide. For most, college is a requirement, and selection requires one where the burden is acceptable.

At any income level there are some who find any burden unacceptable. Others are willing to bear any burden. Others have a misperception of the burden they can actually handle. The American Council on Education regularly has brochures to assist universities in helping families accurately gauge the actual burden.

Pricing strategy is part of the cost perception. A successful pricing strategy is one where none of the potential students within the reach of the university's mission are blocked from attending because of the burden of cost on the family. As with most strategies in the marketing set, this strategy requires that both the actuality and the perception do not cause a block in attendance (Dunn, et al., 1992, 47).

Institutions should do more to emphasize the difference between "list tuition" and "your tuition" without cheapening the institution. The fact is, however, that nearly every person is going to pay a different amount. There are a few institutions that have torn down the walls between the financial aid offices (where the primary concern is safeguarding regulations) and bursar's offices (where the primary concern is collecting the money) to build offices aimed at providing accurate financial counseling—where students are assisted with payment plans, loans, and work opportunities to alleviate the family burden of "their tuition," where their tuition is the amount after external and internal merit and need-based aid is awarded.

Clearly this strategy requires that any calculations of personal tuition amounts be contingent on the accuracy of the financial information given by the student. The institution would be wise also to attempt to guarantee that personal tuition amount, subject to other conditions. Certainty of price information is almost as helpful to lowering the cost barrier as are fat scholarships.

Thus, the goal of the cost element of the marketing strategy is to find a collection of tuition levels, scholarships, and payment plans that bring the financial burden within the perception of "worthwhile" for the family (St. John, 1994, 79). Making the choice "worthwhile," of course depends on the success of other elements of the strategy.

6. **Competitive associations.** Every school has a perceived peer group. Community colleges, Ivy League universities, Seven Sisters, Jesuit universities, state universities, state "flagship" universities all carry perceptual baggage. These associations are the background against which an individual institution must seek differentiation. ("We are the same as our sibling institutions in some ways, but in many, other ways, we are much better.") Few institutions have attempted

to change this perception as part of a marketing strategy. Fewer still have been successful. The University at Albany is still SUNY Albany to me. Most former agricultural colleges have been able to shed that image. Former teachers colleges have a broader image these days, but the group's image has changed fairly uniformly. While all state teachers colleges were viewed similarly in the past, all comprehensive state universities (former state teachers colleges) are still seen as pretty much alike today.

Other transformations have been more dramatic. Many former men's and women's colleges have become coeducational, in most cases making startling transformations in both reality and perception. (See Anderson [1977] for an analysis of the short- and long-term financial consequences of these strategies.) Buena Vista College in Iowa has pushed from obscurity to startling success and has drawn a new set of associated colleges.

7. **Idiosyncrasies.** Differentiation need not be based on the fundamental. A college in rural Maine can have exactly the same academics and pricing as one in Manhattan, but the two are clearly different. While these "extras" can be selling points, their faddish nature requires that market strategies use them only on the margins.

Academic strategies

Like marketing strategies, these orientations must flow from the mission of the college. A book aimed at financial professionals need not spend too much time in this area. Academic disciplines should be viewed as inherently noble and strategic. As such, the institutional process of adding and dropping disciplines must be as informed as any other strategic orientation, if not more.

Academic strategies can be designed in a number of dimensions. Nevertheless, rarely do institutions work to consciously devise an academic strategy in these dimensions. Academic strategies are often the result of a haphazard walk through the political maze of any institution. Departments are strong because of the power and interest of various presidents, provosts, deans, and faculty members. Weak faculty members can allow strong areas to collapse. Ideas of coherency and attention to student needs are themes sounded by new presidents. Social and political histories of curricula are fascinating. I, however, believe that consciously setting a strategic direction, indicated by clear preferences for curriculum change in the dimensions discussed below, will lead to improved integration of academic strategies with the overall strategic direction of the university and will make progress toward mission success more rapid. Some of the dimensions include:

1. **Internal driven or external driven.** St. John's College and many dedicated liberal arts colleges (not "general studies") develop their curriculum based on "received" knowledge. The great books and the basic elements of liberal arts are known. They certainly are not "voted on" by students. Externally driven curricula are less dependent on the canon and more dependent on faculty perception of student needs, requests from advisory groups, and state economic labor shortage forecasts.

   No university is at the end of either spectrum entirely. A university might note which courses are parts of an intrinsic development and which appear to be responses to student needs. The number of credits taken by students from each type might give an overall ex post facto strategic measure. The university might then ask, "Is this really where we want to be?"

2. **Centralized or Decentralized.** An institution that aims at a more centralized academic strategy has "weak" major requirements. All courses are designed to be of interest to all students. Declaring a major does not cut a student off from all other experiences. A decentralized institution, in contrast, allows the creation of majors where few courses outside of that area will be taken. These institutions are where we see "calculus for philosophers" types of courses, offered by the philosophy department. (A budgeting strategy that rewards course points taught can force this parochialism to run rampant.)

   The measure for this strategy is the proportion of course points (students times credits taken) by nonmajors of the total number of course points. This measure can be done two ways: including all "nondeclared" students or excluding these students from the numerator and the denominator. Including them would show how strongly increasing or decreasing the number of nondeclared students affects the centrality measure.

3. **Deep or Shallow.** Deep curricula offer many courses for each major, many more than might be required. Shallow institutions offer fewer courses for each major. This can be put into effect by increased centrality, where students are encouraged to take more courses outside of their major, or by offering courses with larger enrollments and duplicate sections. Clearly this measure is one dimension of the illusive indication of "quality." The measure for this is the ratio of the number of course titles offered within a major to the number of course titles required within the major. The ratios for all majors would be weighted by the numbers of majors and averaged. An increasing ratio over time would indicate increasing depth.

4. **Long or short.** Some institutions have a strategy within a number of disciplines of offering a full list of degrees: associates, bachelors, masters, and doctoral. Sometimes they even offer several types of each within the same discipline. A shorter strategy keeps most offerings at a single degree level with only small excursions at other levels.

   There are two measures of interest. One is oriented toward measuring how long the curriculum is without regard to student activity. The other looks at actual activity. The first is the proportion of available majors that offer degrees at two and three levels (two measures). The second is the proportion of students receiving degrees at the most popular degree level. As this decreases, the institution would appear to be using a "longer" academic strategy.

5. **Skills or content.** Accounting, research methods, and statistics are skills courses. The typical final exam question is: "Can you do this?" History, literature, and sociology are content courses. The typical final exam question for them is: "Do you remember this?" (Both have final exam questions that are: "Do you understand this?")

   This is, in fact, a weak dimension. The effort expended to classify courses may be greater than what we would learn. The strategic question would be, however, whether the drift toward more and more credits for skills courses is part of our strategic plan. Is this what more students seek? Is there a general dissatisfaction with one type of course over another? If the current balance is desired, a strategic plan should not be silent on the split.

6. **Skills or attitude.** I always felt that the academic strategy at the Harvard Business School in this dimension was pure attitude, and I do not mean that disparagingly. The attitudes included a bold approach to problem solving, an assumption of leadership, and a willingness to go beneath the surface of any situation to get at the true causes. These were taught with the case method. If a student did not have a skill, like accounting, it was the student's responsibility to teach it to him or herself. Although the word attitude was never used in a strategic context, skills were regarded as belonging only to inferior beings.

7. **Flashy or meek.** The flashy strategies are usually connected with obtaining "name" professors. Other institutions are chary of loading up with professors who teach only a single, graduate course, have expensive laboratories, and bring uneven external funding. As with all these choices, one strategy does not fit all. In certain circumstances a flashy strategy can work well, as long as the appropriate resources are available for the investment. In other cases, an institution may wish to devise a strategy that retreats from the fancy, but seeks quality along other dimensions.

8. **Professional- or citizen-oriented.** The University of Cincinnati and Northeastern University have excellent cooperative education programs. These programs are part of an academic strategy that prepares graduates for the world of work. Other institutions are less oriented toward specific employment categories and produce students who function well as citizens, scholars, and leaders in a broad range of professions.

    The measure here is the ratio of graduates with degrees clearly aimed at a narrow career area over the total number of degrees. As liberal arts colleges added business majors and MBA programs over the last 30 years, higher education has moved toward narrower career preparation. The next decade may see a drift in the other direction. My question is, do institutions want to follow the trend or lead?

9. **Stable or high churn.** What proportion of courses each year has never been offered before? Is this ratio higher or lower than in the past? What is the trend? A stable curriculum should correlate with an internally driven academic strategy. If the university's academic

strategy, however, is to be responsive to society's needs, then it must be able to add and delete courses and programs with some flexibility. If this indicator is lower than other strategies would call for, then the university may not be putting sufficient resources into the course design and review process.

10. **Thematic or pointillist.** One indicator for this measure of the degree that students may design their own curriculums might be the proportion of courses taken by graduates that are not specifically required for a major or minor: any free elective, or course taken to satisfy a distribution requirement. Courses taken for a major that were not used for graduation because the student switched majors or dropped out should also be included as courses outside of major requirements. The question we are asking is: How many courses are parts of a design and how many are pursued for other reasons?

I apologize if I seem to indicate that student experiment and selection of electives is less than productive. I favor some degree of experimentation and, certainly, there is little research in the area on the effectiveness or ineffectiveness of cafeteria-style academic careers. I would like to know at my institution, however, if we are drifting or designing.

Good strategic development requires debate based on facts like this measure. Do our alumni cite their guided experience or their serendipity as critical to later success? Do we believe we have moved away from a traditional stand that was working? Do we believe that we should be moving away? Is the perception of a cafeteria-style education hurting us?

11. **Faculty-centered or resource-centered.** How many courses are centered on the faculty member through lecture or discussion and how many seem to center on another resource, like library or online research, personal experience, or technology or on facilities, like clinics, studios, or laboratories? At this time, I don't find this dimension terribly interesting. While the faculty role has been changing, their importance has not. They continue to be key to the facilitation of learning. Nevertheless, I anticipate that this may not always be so. As the strengths of technology and our understanding of the learning process shifts, institutions need to recognize that the role of faculty is a strategic pillar.

While this list may be exhausting, it is not exhaustive. Clearly there are enough dimensions in which institutions can develop unique academic strategies and that are appropriate to their missions without copying the successes of others. A fully developed academic strategy will help the campus community understand the rationale for decisions and processes. Hiring and promotion decisions ought to be consonant with the strategy. Course and curriculum development and review processes need to be designed with the strategy in mind. A curriculum development process that does not reward the developers and does not specify all the criteria for acceptance will not allow an institution to be fully responsive to the needs of its constituencies, should it choose to be.

Research strategies

Many universities include a dedication to the discovery and dissemination of knowledge in their missions. These institutions have found that a research strategy evolves over time. If the strategy is found wanting, the strategic dimensions below will illuminate the areas of choice to correct this. The institution can choose to shift into one of these dimensions to create a research strategy more likely to result in a successful approach to the institutional vision.

Strategic thinking requires that university decision makers be ready to ask: "Is there a research strategy?" "Can we articulate it?" "Is it one that is moving the institution toward its vision?" "How might we change it to be more appropriate and successful?" Below are several dimensions of interest:

1. **Opportunistic or planned.** Some universities have few guidelines other than, "Wherever you can get funding." Other universities may develop incentives and prohibitions to more tightly guide the direction of research. The wise strictures of academic freedom prevent most types of prohibitions, except those that compromise the values of the institution. Nevertheless, some institutions wait for the funding and then respond. Others more strongly prepare the infrastructure and bring in personnel strength to establish particular areas of research strength.

   There are risks with both strategies. (See Balderston [1990]) for a discussion of risks with research funding.) With opportunism the chance is high that the response to a large grant or contract will be slow. This makes it difficult for the university to meet deadlines for the completion of a program and for deliverables. In contrast, universities may invest in stellar faculty members and facilities without sufficient grant success to justify the expenditure. In the former case, the lack of planning is cursed. In the latter, it is the dependence on the plan that is cursed.

2. **Centers or departments.** Some universities feature research centers as the primary location for research. With a "center" strategy, universities find it easier to call attention to particular areas of research concentration. A separate center makes it easier to attract research leadership in the area (Balderston, 1995, 122–23). Universities have greater flexibility to reallocate support, should funding decrease. (Nevertheless, I have seen the gold letters on the glass doors stay up far longer than the funding.)

   Putting hurdles in the way of "center creation" keeps research located within departments. This strategy brings research and teaching in closer contact and more easily ensures the employment of graduate students.

3. **Buy or make.** "Buy" here refers to the practice of recruiting researchers to the campus, bringing their grants with them and, it is hoped, securing more. "Make" refers to a strategy of assisting existing faculty members in the pursuit of research funding.

   The "buy" strategy is often used with a more planned approach to research. A new area of research is identified or an existing one is targeted for funding. With insufficient talent in the area, a "buy" strategy must be used.

4. **High incentive or low.** Some universities set aside funds to improve the research infrastructure available to the faculty member, department, division, or the university as a whole. When this is done using proportions of indirect cost recovery income, the faculty member and department are given strong incentives to pursue support.

   However, because indirect cost recovery revenue is calculated as an offset to the increased overhead resulting from the research effort, some support of the costs of doing research is thus being moved to tuition, gifts, state support, and endowment. Students may be unintentionally overburdened to the extent that tuition, for example, is being diverted to research support and covers more than the direct and imputed indirect costs of instruction.

5. **Defense or nondefense.** Some institutions have proscribed certain types of research they deem as contrary to their mission.

6. **Applied or basic.** This is a choice that is determined more by the areas of specialty in which the institution concentrates. Some universities use incentives based on patent license fees and royalties to influence the type of research undertaken.

7. **Funded or unfunded.** Some universities budget their own funds for research. Once again the source of those funds is the crux of the problem. If the research is unfunded, are the actual funders, for example students or the state, fully aware of their support, and are the researchers as accountable for their work as are funded researchers?

Financial strategies

Financial strategies are designed to manage three areas: risk (Dickmeyer, 1982), incentives, and participation. (Pricing strategies, although financial in nature, are discussed under marketing strategies.) The systems where these strategies have an effect are investing (which includes investments in new programs and people), budgeting, and asset management.

1. **Risk.** The basic theory for managing risk with financial strategies is to maximize return within the risk profiles of the governing board and senior administration across all strategies, while recognizing the inherent probability of fluctuation in the environment. Just like industries with lower exposure to consumer product consumption fluctuations—utilities, for example, may take on greater financial risk by borrowing more highly—universities with strong enrollment potential are also allowed to borrow more by financial markets. Financial risk is set by the policies of many areas: financial investing, investing in revenue expansion (fund-raising, recruiting, technology, and new academic programs), contingency budgeting, borrowing, tenure, pricing, and construction. Fluctuations come from cost increases from major burden items (and the more the cost increase of an item, the

larger the burden and the greater risk exposure it represents) and from deviations from expectation from major revenue areas. Also, beyond commonly budgeted areas there is exposure to judgments, settlements, fines, and penalties resulting from litigation and regulatory missteps. Financial strategies need to be sufficiently conservative to balance against these risks (Karol and Ginsburg, 1980, 172–75).

Institutions with small endowments, for example, should invest more conservatively than those with large endowments, even though their dependence on the revenue stream is less, because, generally, their environment is more given to greater fluctuation. Those with a history of enrollment fluctuations, associated with institutions with small endowments, require the offset of a more dependable source of revenue (Rowley and Sherman, 2001, 33).

Investing in the expansion of fund-raising and recruiting may pay off handsomely, in terms both of increased revenue and revenue streams with lower or countercyclical variability. Nevertheless, there is great risk. Not only might these efforts not show the return that would justify them (assuming that a specific return is set as a goal), but they may also spur competitive moves, reducing the return to low levels, and requiring a continued investment. Our strategies in playing this "prisoner's dilemma" game (Miller, 2003, 115–50) have been crude at best. We have yet to declare that only a certain percentage of revenue should be spent on fund-raising, recruiting, or financial aid before it becomes "unseemly." There is not an "economic" solution to the game, yet long-term cooperation in prisoner's dilemma games is demonstrably favorable to both players. The difficulty comes in figuring out how to send the signals to the "prisoner in the other cell" in real life without violating restraint of trade laws. Institutions generally underestimate the risk involved in making these types of investments. We need to move from viewing these as games to maximize individual gain, to games requiring maximization of collective interests (like we do with insurance).

New academic programs are also investments that can increase fixed costs, usually based on an assumption of increased revenue. Institutions should be very careful about the rate of academic program expansion. While there is less likelihood of competitive retaliation, there is the risk that rather than increase enrollments, the enrollments are merely moved around. A careful financial strategy would specify a rate of new program development (and old program phaseout), where the risk was sustainable and fits within the overall financial strategy of the university (Dunn, et al., 1992, 58).

Technology investments share the difficulties mentioned in both paragraphs above. Estimating benefits is extremely difficult, like estimating increased revenue from a new academic program. Institutions also invest in technology in response to competitive moves. In many cases, moving from telephone registration to online registration confers no advantage to the student nor does it improve administrative operations. Yet, the embarrassment of being the last college on the block to offer online registration is more than some institutions can bear. The proportion of expenditures taken up by software and hardware licenses, debt service on technology purchases, maintenance contracts, and specialized technology personnel has increased enormously in the last 15 years. To the extent that these added costs are fixed, financial risk grows.

Contingencies are one of the most direct ways of managing risk (Meisinger and Dubeck, 1984, 100–101). Contingencies show up in institutional and departmental budgets and collectively with insurance. An understanding of the risks inherent in normal tuition revenue fluctuation, student demographics, and costs drives the necessity of contingencies. Contingencies can be partially replaced or enhanced by budgeting strategies that slowly release discretionary funds or that clearly outline the cuts that will be made should revenues not meet expectations early in the year.

Abuse of contingencies undermines carefully constructed financial strategy. In some cases it may be necessary to restrict spending authorization from contingencies to the finance committee of the board. Use of contingencies early in the fiscal year for presidentially approved discretionary items demonstrates a lack of understanding of the use of contingencies to buffer risk. The development of contingencies within the budget process is a good example of everyday strategic thinking, sometimes only lacking a more careful examination of risk and fluctuation to properly place the decision in a strategic context.

To the extent that debt increases fixed costs (especially since the costs are generally owed to especially powerful actors, like banks), borrowing increases risk. While the proportion of expenditures locked into debt service may be small compared to salaries and benefits for tenured faculty, it's the combination of the two that represents risk. Both represent commitments that are slow to decline in the face of negative revenue trends. Both generally represent investments to improve or secure revenue. Borrowing is at least self-limiting; in that lenders look at the degree of risk and first raise rates, then shy away.

Institutions in more stable financial environments should be able to devise a strategic approach to risk that allows higher debt levels and a higher proportion of tenured faculty. This seemed to be the strategy of public universities with very high proportions of tenured faculty, compared with private institutions. Let us see if public institutions search for strategies to lower the proportion of the budget spent on tenured faculty salaries in the face of the great increase in fluctuations in state support.

Institutions engage in leverage with their institutional financial aid policies (McPherson and Winston, 1992, 74). Leverage generally means increased dependence on a single source and, hence, greater risk. Institutions following a pricing policy of large increases to tuition with even larger increases to need-based aid tend to be shifting a larger proportion of revenue to a smaller and smaller group of people: the "full payers." As tuition goes up, the number of students who do not qualify for aid decreases. The revenue coming from those on aid is fixed at what the formula says they can pay. Only the full payers contribute to the increase from increased tuition prices. As the number of full payers decreases with increasing tuition price, the risk of losing this group of students also increases. Thus, certain pricing strategies directly contribute to increased risk and must be taken into consideration when developing a risk-aware financial strategy (Dickmeyer, 1993, and Hauptman, 1992, 127).

Construction brings with it more than the risks of new debt. Construction also brings fixed costs required for running and maintaining a building. Few buildings come with endowments large enough to pay for janitors, security officers, utilities, and regular renovation. An increase in floor space automatically plunges more of the budget into the fixed category.

Developing a financial strategy that balances all these risks against the inherent risks of the environment is undertaken in the regular cycles of budgeting, program evaluation, endowment investment development, and fixed asset investment decisions and insuring.

2. **Incentives and sanctions.** Besides managing risk, financial strategies are needed that explicitly consider how financial incentives and sanctions change behavior. The strategic choice is to find the proper combination of sanctions and incentives. A strategy built on low sanctions and low incentives can lead to anarchy in the form of budget overspending, inefficiency, and inattention to priorities. A strategy of high sanctions and high incentives may appear to be contradictory, but all types of personalities are likely to respond well. An exaggeration of such a strategy would include full responsibility for budgeting a large portion of earned revenues and demotion or suspension for failure to stay within the revenue limits.

I've always enjoyed the apocryphal story of the dean who every year overspent earned revenues on supplies three-quarters of the way through the year, requiring a university subvention to support salaries to the end of the year. As punishment they made him provost.

Among the behaviors that financial incentive/sanction strategies attempt to manage are budget control, revenue solicitation, end of year spending, new program budgeting, budget reallocation and efficiency, pursuit of research funding, and attention to strategic priorities. For each of these areas, the university may define behaviors more conducive to success on the mission. Success is not necessarily equivalent to maintaining complete control. Complete control may force movement in the desired direction, but forced movement is usually slow, begrudging, and easily retracted.

Make sure that the incentives and sanctions are based on measurable behaviors over which managers have control. It would make little sense to penalize Arts and Sciences because the library overspent its budget. Nevertheless, burdening Arts and Sciences with an arbitrary allocation of library expenses as an indirect cost is equivalent. Conversely, if the library's spending is strongly related to demands by Arts and Sciences, then the measure makes sense.

These strategies must have a cultural base. A change to a new strategy, based on strong incentives, must be accomplished gradually and with much participation (Rowley and Sherman, 2001, 185). While many people will call for greater freedom in financial decision making, rarely is everyone ready for the responsibility, nor will they all comprehend the full implications of the change. Nevertheless, the movement away from centralized planning because of the limited understanding by central managers of all decentralized functions (March and Simon, 1958, 203) requires the substitution of some level of centrally managed incentives and sanctions.

For example, responsibility-center budgeting implies a large amount of control over revenues on the part of the unit or center (Meisinger and Dubeck, 1984, 188–89, and Whalen, 1991, 10). This may be true of a school in a university, where even tuition prices may be set and where fund-raising is undertaken in coordination with, but separately, from the central administration. Translating this concept to a department in a small college can only be done with difficulty. The department depends to a great degree on central offices, even when managing enrollment levels.

A strategy that is heavy on incentives relies on rational market behavior. Those that do well in the marketplace may get larger budgets or the ability to spend fixed budgets with more discretion. Winners can also get space, parking, and titles.

Areas that generate more revenues are able to keep all or a portion of the extra revenues (Meisinger, 1994, 186–87). The hard question is what to do with those areas that fall below revenue expectations. Do we tell the School of Social Work to shut down in April because they have run out of money? Dedication to the purposes of the School of Social Work require that it be kept going. Wealthier schools must be taxed to support it. A dual case must be made for such support, however. The school must prove its value in the context of the university's mission, and it must prove that bad management is not the cause of the problems. The school needs to show that the problems are caused by temporary, unfortunate market conditions. Even in large universities there are some units that are too small to have much control over their financial fate.

Space can be subject to market play as a part of a heavy incentive strategy (Massy and Meyerson, 1992, 18). Funds currently budgeted for depreciation, maintenance, and renovation reserves can be reallocated on a revenue-sensitive basis, like enrollments with a heavier weighting for graduate enrollments to each department. The same amount in total that is allocated as a budget increase to the departments can be allocated as an expense to departments on a square foot basis. There are many, many degrees of sophistication that should be added to this to allow for public space and usage intensities, but the result is generally something of an imbalance for those departments with large tracts and low enrollments. If the allocation is phased in over several years, these space-rich departments realize they are losing discretionary budget unless they can get some of their space assigned to general use. While space-poor departments may pick up an extra professor at the expense of the supply budgets of the space rich departments, in general, the university has a net gain as the demand for additional space decreases with better use.

End-of-the-year spending patterns can also be managed with incentives. In some institutions budgets must be spent by the end of the year. This often brings about a flurry of last-minute spending to prevent a loss of "perfectly good budget funding" (Balderston, 1995, 163–64). In some universities the practice of decreasing budgets in areas of underspending punishes budget control. Allowing a carry forward of all, or a portion, of unspent funds makes for much more careful buying practices. In some states, this is not possible, because there is no allowable carry forward. At the extreme of control, to prevent a bit of last-minute spending, a large team of auditors is assembled to count toilet tissue and pens. Obviously a strategy of market-based incentives is incompatible with a philosophy of bureaucratic control.

Allowing some form of carry forward is an excellent example of an "action" strategy. A strategic-planning document cannot change behavior and move an institution nearly as well as a well-developed incentive.

3. **Participation.** The final dimension of financial strategies is the orientation toward participation. The choices range from autocracy to anarchy. In an autocratic administration, the method is "budgeting by begging." In anarchy, no one takes responsibility. A methodology must be developed well in the middle.

Making the budget requires technical skills, but the budget makers must be accountable to all constituencies for a budget that moves the institution toward its strategic goals. Participation should be heavy at the strategic level and light at the technical level, but the technicians must be accountable.

Participation can mean advising, or it can mean deciding. Suggesting that participation might mean deciding and then refusing to follow the preference can be devastating for an administration. Moving the discussion of and setting the charge to the budget committee at the level of strategies and away from the number of secretaries for the French department may be the best way to bring in meaningful participation. A request to develop financial strategies with higher risk and return levels and to move toward the use of more incentives, or even one to build science learning, is much easier to work with than one to hire six more physics professors.

Strategies of greater participation rest on getting out more financial information and analyses and an effort to make the budget transparent. They also rest on elevating the level of debate above that of payoffs for good behavior to real trade-offs within real constraints. Financial models can be used to elevate language. This can be an important preface to change (Eckel and Kezar, 2003, 42).

To the extent that decisionmaking is not delegated downward, however, greater participation requires that ideas and suggestions be taken seriously and responded to, especially if responded to negatively, with thorough analyses. Strategies that move toward greater participation require greater investment in time and analysis to work. The payoff may be in greater effort toward strategic goals and decreased tension. Nevertheless, greater participation as a strategy is not costless.

Currently financial strategies are being developed outside of strategic planning projects. They are made "on the run and live." Strategic thinking is part of what we, as CFOs, do all day in these areas as we develop budget processes, write reports, allocate space, spend and invest endowment, and repair the plant. The more we can put these strategies in the context of all our strategies, the better all will work. Conservative budgeting processes are going to get tangled up in an entrepreneurial academic arena. It is not so much this year's budget but this year's budget process that is an indicator of the strategic designs coming out of the financial area, as will be discussed in chapter 11 on integrating budgeting planning and the budget.

Community strategies

The depth of the relationship between the institution and the "outer world" should be viewed as a strategy derived from the mission and in consonance with the strategies previously developed. The extremes are manageable in this case with well-known examples of institutions deeply mingled with the affairs and lives of the community and those that are completely aloof. The deeply integrated colleges perhaps hold the values of their community more strongly than those of academe, risking approbation of accreditors and the American Association of University Professors (AAUP) alike. The aloof hold academe's values so tightly that they risk the wrath of the community.

The mission is the guide. The more closely the university pledges service to its neighbors and the world, the more the community strategy needs expression in all its aspects. My local community college reaches out with honors programs for the shy, plays and music for the cultured, artistic courses for the idle, and boat shows for the rest. Jesuit university faculty members and priests set the example of service to all with crowds of students venturing into the ghettos for enduring volunteer efforts.

Service should not be an afterthought tacked onto academics. Service is an expression of the intent of the institution, be it isolation or integration. The service strategy should not be designed by a separate office of volunteers, but it should be a part of the strategic design for the institution.

The spirit of the place should require that daily decisions include the questions "How will this affect the community?" and "How can this decision be done to have a positive effect on the community in line with our community strategy?" Included should be the question "How can I learn more about the needs of the community in the areas that might be affected by this question?"

Day-to-day decisionmaking must reflect accountability for each decision's impact on the community. How has the community been informed of the issue? How have they been asked to participate and voice their concerns? How has the institution been responsive? What has been done to assure the community that the university's long-range plan has taken their needs into consideration? What evidence has the institution given that it has concern for the community?

Some institutions feel few obligations toward their community. Their politics have been those of power, and they have offered consolation only after winning. Other institutions have the trust and support of the community, often allied against other political structures in the city. The difference is the difference between viewing community affairs as the project of a separate office and viewing it as a daily concern of all members of the college community. This is also the difference between a strategic planning project and strategic thinking. The responsibility for attending to the strategic direction of the university is completely on each member of the college community, and each member must attend to it daily. The strategy must spell out for them the principles of behavior in making decisions that have a hint of impact on the community.

Let us take one area: hiring. Employment at the university is a privilege for those qualified to perform beyond the high ideals of each occupation. Nevertheless, a university that espouses a strong obligation to the community develops visible career ladders that allow employees to enter from the community, gain skills and experience, and move up at a pace that does not climb too fast, leading to failure. Jobs need to be carefully described in a way that admits the broad range of people from the community. Too often job descriptions are written from the point of view of the writer or the incumbent, not allowing that the job, with small modification, could be done by someone with a disability or gap in training or experience.

Hiring is not just a door into the university. It is a link to the community. Reaching out through that door to assist in the education of youths and in programs to sharpen young ideas about the world ahead of them is part of a community strategy that acknowledges that link. Many institutions have developed that concept very carefully and draw with them a community strengthened through their efforts. These institutions draw the best from afar as well. Their concern for and depth of experience in the community brings to them the best of those so committed. Affirmative action is not just an office and a plan. It is proven in the efforts of the college outside of the interview room.

Service strategies

How shall I serve thee? A strategic orientation is needed on service. For each office that deals with students and faculty and other staff members, the simple motto, "We give good service," is insufficient. The institution needs to view the interchange between it and all members of the university community, whether it is person to person, over the phone to a person, or via the Web to a person, as the daily carrying out of a primary strategy. The range of possible behaviors highlights the strategic nature of this area from "jiffy rude" to empathy and efficiency. The strategic nature of this area is also given by the critical importance of success before mission success is possible. An institution that neglects its clients and allows daily insults to its frontline staff can never be effective at serving its clients as hoped for in the mission statement.

Elevating service to a strategy for moving the institution to success brings it beyond the workshop exercises offered by once-a-year customer service training. These workshops may still be part of the strategy, but all people in the university community need to see how the effort of the workshop ties to strategically fulfilling the mission of the institution. Like most strategic designs, the service strategy needs to dwell on how people are to be treated and why. How should people feel after we have rendered service? Why do we want that to happen? What makes this strategic?

Like academic strategies, service strategies need to be built within the resources available. Hundreds of open phone lines are not going to be possible, but the service strategy must still leave the client feeling the evidence of the strategy. This is a sample strategic development statement:

Our strategy has been to place the human interchange on a level with the growth of the human intellect. That is, we have sought to understand and define the terms of each type of interchange in a way that would leave both parties improved. For our staff this has meant that they have sought to better understand the needs of each person being assisted, to become gifted in the ways of perceiving needs. For our clients, we have sought to give not only better understanding of how they can deal with their situations and the tools to do so, but also the understanding that we do so with careful attention and concern for them.

This imperfectly conceived strategy has, nonetheless, enormous implications for staff development and practice. Few institutions can afford the full drama of training for this. The implications are also there that in some cases the interchange may go beyond the level of skills acquitted a staff member. More skilled administrators may need to be called in before the frustration of failure is upon the staff member.

This sample strategy is at a fair extreme. Less overreaching examples abound that nonetheless give coherence to the overall set of strategies of the institution. Once again, the strategy is not a set of rules, but a way of daily behaving that evidences a way of moving the institution toward its goals.

THE PROCESS

In the end, however, all we have from the above is a grand list of ideas. We still do not have a process for developing the set of strategies on which we must concentrate. We are back to where we started in this chapter, because the list is the result of a deductive analytic process and the only comprehensive process for strategic development is inductive. We are required to examine many, many ideas to find a few that are to be applied in daily work. This can be done with a high level of participation, using a community Web page structure. All constituencies should be invited to participate, while a responsible team reacts to the ideas and begins to build a strategy.

The Web page needs to have links to these items:

1. Here is our mission today.
2. Here is a statistical picture of what we are now.
3. Here is the vision of what we would like to be in 5 (10?) years.
4. Here is what our competition looks like.
5. Here are important trends happening around us.
6. Here are all the strategies that we might use (from the framework above).
7. Which strategies would we judge to be the most important in the effort to change us from what we are now to our vision and why?
    a. How will these strategies differentiate us from our competitors?
    b. How will these strategies help us garner resources to implement our vision?

It is the daily building of the ideas in this Web page and organizing online teams to do so that will allow the institution to move toward a focused set of strategies, selected as giving the most leverage toward success. It may take several years to build the initial links to the point where the strategic discussion can be made, but the road to strategic thought is long. Strategic thought comes from daily attention to the environment and competitors. It comes from continually refining the vision and regular appraisal of the adequacy of the mission. It comes from a hard focus on a few strategic elements that themselves are under constant scrutiny for their fit to the evolving challenges of the environment.

Many strategic elements will come up in the discussion that will have to be relegated to the "of course" holding pen. These are strategic elements that have always been important and will continue to be important to the institution, but regardless of the level of conscious emphasis, they will not change the institution. Change, move, push, shove, lift and turn, twist, and shake are the operative verbs. We need a set of strategies that will change the institution. These are the ones that deserve our focus.

A Day in the Life: Faith Quentin,
Director of Admissions, Atwell Richards College

Closing the last folder on her desk, Faith picked up the stack and glanced out of her window at the sun setting on the Hiawatha River in northern Iowa. She walked out of her office and put the pile in the center of her assistant's nicely cleared desk. Because it was well after 6:00 p.m., she knew that she need not feel guilty. Yet, she knew in the morning, William's cheerful, "Thanks. I will take care of these right now," was going to be more than she wanted to hear.

"One last thing," she thought, going back into her office and logging onto the college's strategic planning site. She had gotten an e-mail from the president, advising her to check the "New Student Recruitment" page, where a stream of comments were coming in. Faith was chair of the "New Student Recruiting Strategy Committee," and she knew that the president wanted her to react to today's comments.

After surfing to the comments from today, she noticed that the day began with a long essay from the president, posted at 6:30 a.m. "Typical," she mumbled. He was always first to the keyboard in the morning.

The president was in his first year and was enjoying great popularity with the board and faculty. A very hard worker, he was in the office early and out in the social whirl late. He spent much of his time walking on campus, eating in the cafeteria with the students, and going to see faculty members in their offices. He even had a one-hour slot each week available for Faith to schedule new student parents to come and see him. Faith knew how to pick out those parents who were wavering about the college, and she could count on a visit with the president to win them over.

She began reading the president's words. "After spending much time with many of the fine faculty, staff, and students here at ARC, I am convinced that our primary strategy for the future is to aim to become the Harvard on the Hiawatha." Faith leaned back in her chair, closed her eyes and murmured, "Oh no! Here we go again."

She was remembering 12 years ago when another new president pushed in the same direction. Enrollments plunged from 8,000 to 3,500 and 20 percent of the faculty members were laid off, with extremely hard feelings. The board realized their mistake—but very late—and finally brought in a new president. The first thing the new president did was to hire Faith, because of her fine record at a for-profit school, and told her, "Bring in the students. I don't care how. Just bring in the students."

Those were the days. Faith would find a market, and the president would build a matching program. If there were interest in graphic arts, the college would build a program. If veterinarians needed technicians, the college built a program. If the Troyton police stopped the president for speeding, the next thing you knew the college had a 20 percent discount program for Troyton city employees.

She read on. The president noted that what ARC lacked was a house system in the residence halls, tougher admissions standards, scholarships for Iowa valedictorians, a faculty-mentoring program, a new student center, research grants, and varsity crew. She then skimmed the comments that followed. As she suspected, she found 14 endorsements from faculty on the idea in the stream. Isabella Page in English had three separate favorable comments, but then, that's Isabella. She knew some were holding back, fearful of offending the new president by reminding people about the earlier experience.

She was torn about what to reply. There certainly would be some truth to any comments that she didn't like the idea because that was not her professional strength. She was good at bringing in students from first-generation-college families. This is always a challenge for private institutions, but she knew that the college had a lot to offer these students. She knew what their fears were and how to calm them. So, yes, the Harvard stuff would not be her forte.

"Well, if we are going to go down in flames, let's at least be professional about it," she thought. She began typing.

"If we are looking for a strategic idea that could pick us up and point us in a new direction, the president has hit on it. By defining a new experience for our students, the president has defined a new market, new ways of serving our students, and new standards of performance for all of us. There is no question that this strategy has implications from lawn care to library collections.

"To be really successful with this strategy we will need to understand the new market that we will be exploring. In a 100-mile radius, there are 17 colleges: 15 private and 2 public institutions. Currently, we offer the lowest tuition among all the private colleges, except one career-oriented for-profit. Among the 15, 4 have annual tuition in excess of $16,000 and have reputations for good quality. I am supposing that our aim should be to be as good, or better than these four colleges. If our strategy is successful, we should be able to create a distinctive college that could draw enrollment from these four schools.

"From the reports I do on our recruiting success, I note that our new student market share among the 15 colleges has grown from 7 percent to 12 percent in the last four years. I also note that the combined market share of the four top-rated schools has dropped from 10 percent to 9 percent in the last four years. So, if we replaced all of our freshmen with all of theirs, we would have fewer students, but they would, of course, be paying a higher tuition. Let's say I am not entirely comfortable with this first-pass analysis of market potential for this strategy.

"Good strategies are both successful in the competitive market and build on strength. ARC has much strength. Does this strategy build on our strength? In the last four years, we have recruited three valedictorians. One dropped out in the first month. One transferred after one semester and one is still with us. She loves it here and works in my office. One out of three may not give us much statistical significance, and batting .333 is pretty good in baseball. . . .

"I am wondering if the president would like to shift the strategy to one of treating our students like Harvard students. I think many of his ideas can be used to build on the strengths we have now, including the strategic way that we are now serving the region."

With this she logged off. She got up, walked over to the light switch, and mumbled to herself, "Well, I'll probably get fired either way. Either because I can't get students his way, or because I called his idea 'dumb.'" She hit the switch and walked out the door.

Seven Key Thoughts

1. Do not expect that a cookbook approach to strategic development will work well. Strategic thought is inductive. Strategies must be induced from a welter of theories and data points about success, not deducted from a given theory.

2. Strategies can grow out of many areas of institutional endeavor: marketing, academic, research, financial, community support, and service.

3. Inductive processes require broad participation. As an inductive process, the strategic thought development process can be greatly assisted by online chat methodologies.

4. The answer to "How are we going to make a big change at this university?" is through strategies. The question of what methodology we will use to change in order to reach our vision is answered by a set of strategies.

5. The choice among strategic options requires data. Developing each strategic area requires much conceptual knowledge and data about effectiveness.

6. A collection of strategies must be compatible. The various institutional strategies must not be in conflict. The risk inherent in a marketing strategy should be balanced with the risk in a financial strategy.

7. Service and community strategies may not be primary, but progress requires strategic thought. How to approach and work with the community and how to provide appropriate service levels to students and other constituencies are highly amenable to strategic design.

Chapter Eleven
INTEGRATING PLANNING AND DECISIONMAKING

Much of this book to this point has focused on methods for developing university strategic direction. We can put these methods into operation to enable an understanding of strategic direction to become a part of our daily university work life and to help us avoid making strategic thinking just a planning project. How should our day-to-day management change to effectively put strategic thinking to work? How can we evaluate whether we are using the lessons of strategic thinking every day?

Kaplan and Norton (2001, 1) emphasize that "executing strategy" benefits an organization more than simply having strategies. They also point out how much more challenging implementation is than development.

The life of work for a CFO involves making decisions, designing processes, following personnel procedures and actions, interpreting policies, negotiating on everything, and motivating the people around him or her. These working actions must be undertaken within the framework of institutional strategy. These working actions are the foreground of work life. In the background is the continual revision and refinement of the strategic vision. Much of what goes on in the background consists of task-group assessment of the competitive environment, the regulatory environment, market definition, strategic design, and institutional strengths (Waggaman, 1991, 95).

BACKGROUND: THE PLANNING PROCESS

As will be discussed more in this chapter's special section on linking planning and budgets, the model I propose for planning involves the use of virtual committees. These are groups of people charged with particular tasks that meet using distance-learning, asynchronous technology. The sessions are continuous and use streaming dialogues. A committee chair or editor moderates the committees and the dialogues.

The Mission Task Force. The model proposed here requires that a group be charged with regularly assessing whether the service populations targeted by the mission are changing or should change. This group would also assess whether the institution was living up to the level of service proposed in the mission. The group would then verify that the declared institutional strengths in the mission were of the proper scope and quality level. Finally, these strengths would also require monitoring.

For example, an institution dedicated "to providing excellent health professionals to underserved populations" would need to regularly assess the meaning of "underserved populations." This institution would need to determine if competitive changes or other opportunities meant that other populations could also be included without decreasing the university's intended effect on underserved populations. In this example, the university might also examine whether preparing health professionals alone was sufficient to serve the intended population and whether they could or should pull together the resources needed to broaden their mission.

Such a committee would need members with institutional research and recruiting skills. It would also need the leadership of a president, although another person could be the chair/editor for the virtual committee. Faculty members who understood the basic strengths of the institution would also be an excellent resource for this committee.

Vision Task Force. While development of the institutional vision is largely the responsibility of the president, the president needs support and a sounding board. Virtual committee work is ideal for this, especially since the committee may only need to go over the vision once a year after the vision's original development.

This group would be charged with making sure that the vision is sufficiently concrete and that the vision has enough facets to be useful for the decisions and challenges of the day. For example, if the institution faces declining government support, it needs to be able to define a future direction. Should it hire more lobbyists to fight for improved support or should it design a future as merely, "state affiliated"? The planning process will assist in making that decision, but once the direction is set, the president must be able to say, for example, "I see a college with strength in fund-raising and the ability to set its own tuitions such that fluctuating state support will not have an effect on educational quality."

Environmental realities, the vision, the strategy, and decisions all interact. No one area comes first. Sometimes the vision leads; sometimes the strategy leads. Successful planning can only occur when the institution has the mechanisms in place to be flexible. One such mechanism is the vision task force.

Strategy Leadership Team. As outlined in the previous chapter, there are a large number of areas where strategies may be developed. A leadership team is needed that integrates the strategies that are being built in each of these areas.

An organization may not be successful if the recruiting strategy is to target C+ high school graduates, but the academic offering strategy is to provide "excellent, demanding liberal arts." These two strategies do not integrate well.

This group must also provide the charges to each of the task forces working on the specialized strategies. What must the financial risk strategies task force do? The strategy leadership team would give it a charge, for example, to devise guidelines for endowment investment, debt levels, and contingency budget levels that fit trustee risk profiles and the inherent risks in the environment. Environmental risks can be measured in terms of enrollment fluctuations, tuition dependency levels, governmental support fluctuations, federal student aid fluctuations, gift fluctuations, market fluctuations, and the dependency on these and other sources of support. This committee might work with a strategic consultant to help specialty teams coordinate their efforts and to help in defining the types of strategies that need to be knit together.

Strategic Specialty Teams. As indicated earlier in this chapter, there can be quite a number of these teams. In an ideal situation, every permanent member of the university community should have a chance to serve on one of these committees every few years. Less permanent institutional members, like students, community members, part-time faculty, and part-time staff could also be asked to contribute. Nevertheless, each permanent member of the community, at least, should be asked to spend a few minutes every day thinking about strategy and reacting to the ideas of others. While the CFO would be a continuing member of the financial risk strategy team, other financial staff members should also experience the challenge of devising a set of guidelines for financial decisions that mesh with recruiting/market strategies, environmental fluctuations, and leadership risk preferences.

Without virtual meeting technology the institution would grind to a halt, from either a lack of productivity or burnout. While many of the teams can decrease activity during more demanding times like early fall semester and budget crunch, other teams are engaging in work that goes on regularly. Recruiting strategic development and the operationalization of recruiting strategies proceed hand in hand during most of the year. Having a recruiting strategy team merely formalizes a current endeavor and folds it into the planning process.

The Values Team. Every institution needs a values czar or czarina guided by a team that acts as a sounding board and that understands institutional history and myth. Values guide the "in what way" part of strategic development. Why does this mission fit? What is it about the way we do things and the way we treat people that makes us different, makes us successful, and brings fit to individuals and the organization?

All universities value learning, but some measure success in terms of the high quality of graduates, while others value the growth of individuals during the educational process. Most institutions pride themselves in removing blocks to gaining an education. Many, however, specialize by concentrating on removing one or more particular blocks: financial blocks, language blocks, prior educational quality blocks, location blocks, and/or mobility blocks. Almost all concentrate on removing the blocks of prejudice. Nevertheless, although many concentrate on removing the blocks of racial prejudice, not all have successfully focused on gender or disability prejudice.

In a broad sense, the values are similar, but under careful scrutiny, not all institutions have the resources, history, or will to remove all blocks to gaining an education. Nevertheless, a variety of institutions, each concentrating on what it does best and wants to do best, will lower barriers to all. Without values clarification, ratification, and implementation through the strategic planning process, these ideas turn to mush and the opportunity to pursue them drifts away.

Environmental Assessment Leadership Team. What aspects of the environment bear watching? Regulations, state funding/political moods, economic shifts, market demographics, competition, and foundation preferences all influence the future in which the strategic plan is supposed to fit. The charge of the environmental assessment leadership team is to assess what is important in all this information, to feed digests to the community, and to channel details to those strategic groups that need to know the various findings. This team guides the scanning task forces.

Like understanding and viewing the organization in terms of strategies, understanding and viewing the organization in terms of the environment should be a part of every university member's day (Rowley and Sherman, 2001, 166). This committee would coordinate the efforts of task forces that watch and consider trends in regulations, the economy, and the competition, for example.

Scanning Task Forces. The core of a task force dedicated to watching the economy, for example, might be made up of the CFO, a trustee with a financial interest, and an economics faculty member. Other members from the faculty, staff, and students could provide insights from their connections and interests. Each member should volunteer to peruse particular online publications to look for articles of relevance to the situation of the institution. Some institutions ride the unemployment wave, enrolling more when times are hard. These institutions need to watch and understand leading economic indicators, for example. One person could be charged with tracking and presenting these figures in terms of the probable impact on the institution.

Industry contractions may signal opportunities to support retraining efforts. Understanding wage trends and family income shifts should help with setting pricing and salary strategies. In California, before Enron, it was important, for example, to understand Sierra snowfall to predict electricity prices. By spreading the chores of environmental scanning to members of virtual committees, from watching unemployment to checking competitive shifts, the institution not only brings vital information to strategic development, it also allows individuals to raise their heads above the day-to-day demands of work (Waggaman, 1991, 96–97).

Virtual meetings and e-mail list distribution of committee findings can break down the inefficiencies in current planning methodologies. Presenting drafts of ideas on the Web and allowing the entire community to contribute remove much of the isolation of previous strategic development processes.

FOREGROUND: DOING

A good example of a set of decisions that regularly pops into the foreground are pricing decisions. In a few states, these decisions for public universities are made entirely at the state level. In all private universities and most public institutions, pricing is a difficult set of decisions that must be made in a strategic context. The pricing decision includes setting gross tuition, setting tuition discount policies for various groups, developing formulas for need-based aid, devising policies for awarding non-need aid, and setting guidelines for any price negotiations (for example, shifting need-based awards outside of the policy). Pricing decisions need to accurately reflect market and financial strategies. A strategic decision to serve lower-income students within a higher-risk financial strategy can be pursued by setting moderate tuitions and devising need-based financial aid-packaging formulas that meet most need. We are also seeing "prestige" marketing strategies coupled with higher-risk financial strategies where the institution has a very high tuition and meets all need by using only institutional grants and no loans.

Another set of loosely related decisions has to do with timing. When do courses start and end? We have seen universities that allow only semester-long courses in a strict trimester regimen. We have also seen those with 36 different semester start dates: 16-week courses, 8-week courses, special summer starts for teachers, weekend courses, and so forth. Others have an infinite number of start and stop combinations with self-paced study. Making these decisions within a strategic direction wraps them around the intended markets. Students right out of high school start as a cohort in the fall. Working adults want to start nearly as soon as they make the decision to begin or continue their education, which could be at any time.

We begin by realizing that we need a context for decisions and policies (Dunn, et al., 1992, 40). Whenever we set a tuition rate, devise a need-based student financial aid structure, set salaries, introduce new programs, fund research, set payout rates for the endowment, give risk-level guidance to investment managers, tenure faculty, hire staff, describe job functions, send a former student to collections, forgive a debt, invest in a computing system, plan a building, or float a bond, we do so within a framework that allows us to judge whether the action we propose is good for the university. Let us move planning, doing, and linking into the every day.

Integrating strategic metrics. While we might begin the day on our computer looking at and contributing to task-force activities, we might end the day in contemplation. Every day we need to ask ourselves, "Did the decisions I made today fit within our strategies?" The problem with requiring that we reflect a strategic orientation during decisionmaking is that we seldom realize we are actually in a *decision situation* when we are making or participating in a decision. We shape our days much more than we cut and slice them. As discussed earlier, decisions are usually very long, very social processes without a clear beginning or end. That's why it is important at the end of the day to sharpen our understanding of how we influenced actions (sometimes called decisions) and how that effort relates to our strategic stance.

A bit of time reflecting on a hiring decision in the light of the institution's strategy to remain affordable can be worthwhile. Affordability as a strategy can only be achieved through an efficient use of resources. Does hiring serve this goal or another? Is the other goal as important strategically? Does the decision reflect full appreciation of the strategy? Perhaps it demonstrates a problem with the strategy? Is "What is really important or not" even part of strategic thinking at the institution? Am I out of line with the institutional strategy?

Another benefit of this time of reflection is a stronger awareness of decisions as influence points in day-to-day work. All members of the organization influence the course of the institution: some in major ways, others in small ways. Fully realizing the paths of these influences and noting the course of decisions through the organization highlights the points where individuals and individual strategic orientations move the organization toward or away from its goals.

Besides viewing decisions in the context of strategies, one can also do the opposite. Strategies can be viewed in the context of the day's decisions. How do they stand up? Can I find any evidence of our affordability strategy in anything that I did today? Are other strategies more evident? Should these other strategies be more carefully examined at any level in strategic thinking? Does a day of redesigning student financial assistance show evidence of greater pressure on the institution to be price competitive? Is this clearly a strategy or has it escaped attention?

This daily exercise can be fostered with a small list of measures that show strategic alignment. A strategy to better serve and increase adult participation in higher education calls for an "adult fit" metric. A move to increase the number of evenings the financial services office is open fits adults. Increasing funding for on-campus student jobs probably does not.

Vision metrics. Along with the strategic metrics, the addition of a few metrics that show progress toward the vision can also be helpful. "I see a college that touches the lives of everyone in the community." The metric must be the number of people touched. A proposal to provide summer financial office work experience to two Upward Bound students is probably a step in the right direction.

Value metrics. Finally, add in a few metrics on the way things are done. For example, the faculty senate could prepare a "civility index" based on the number of times ad hominem arguments are used. Staff turnover rates are another possible measure. In some cases, the proportion of faculty and staff affiliated with community organizations would be a useful indicator.

The CFO can also gauge her or his personal value alignment with end-of-day questions like "Did I help the organization learn and remember something important today?" "Did I do something that will remove a barrier to education today?"

The Chief Learning Officer. As an organization dedicated to learning, the university probably already has someone with this role. This is the person in charge of assessing student learning. The person in charge of tracking organizational learning probably reports to the chief learning officer (CLO). If superior learning methodologies and student learning success are what distinguishes this university from others, much of the success of the university obviously rests on the CLO.

The three things game. Here's another exercise that's good to start the day (or something to write down at the end of the day to clear your mind and to start the next day).

1. What three things could I do today that will provide the most leverage for moving the university toward its goals? Leverage means the most movement for the effort. We all ask ourselves, "What fire must I put out now?" We do not view our efforts, however, as having a consequence for moving the institution toward its goals. Haven't we all noticed how many fires get put out while we are on vacation—without

our help? Could we evaluate our efforts more in terms of what is good for the institution, instead of some other, external metric?

2. What three decisions should I work on today? With this you are asking yourself, "How can I be influential?"

3. What three strategies should I keep in mind today? This is just another attempt to bring thoughts of the future and desired consequences more into conscious consideration.

4. What three opportunities did I see yesterday that I should explore further today? This is an attempt to push aside the laziness of having to deal with new situations. Opportunities appear, but we seldom give them a second thought.

5. Which three challenges from yesterday had I better sharpen my recognition of? This is an attempt to bring the scary parts of the future out of denial.

LINKING PLANNING AND DOING

Linking planning and doing means much more than just first making a plan and then carrying it out. Linking means that planning and doing should be done simultaneously with the wisdom gained from the one carried over to the other. That is, decisions, budgets, personnel selection, and choices of what to do and not to do each day must be done within the framework of the strategic direction of the university.

Likewise, planning needs to be done with an awareness of the daily choices that are made. Otherwise the plans become too abstract to have an influence on daily choices. Strategic direction must be set with an awareness that personnel decisions are made, for example. Managers choose people and training experiences. Strategic plans must have something to say about the strengths people should have to contribute strongly to the organization. Choices of people and training experiences should reflect an understanding of these strategic requirements.

An organization that values flexibility in meeting the needs of its clients can develop that idea into a major strategic initiative. The strategic thinking may go so far as to value people who are more than just unafraid of change. The strategic process may reveal that organizational success depends on people who actually welcome change and who are risk takers and careful experimenters. The explicit development of this strategy and these values becomes a goal of finding and developing people with a particular set of traits. This then means that personnel decisions and the selections of training experiences can be made with a direct reference to a strategic initiative. Linking planning and doing occurs when both activities are carried on simultaneously or iteratively, with each process reflecting ideas from the other.

Linking means giving a focus to planning that says, "What does our hope for the future mean for our actions today?" At the same time, it means giving a rational justification for our actions by providing the logic of purpose. An understanding of our range of choices, influences, and actions moves planning from the abstract to the concrete. A framework of intention moves our actions from the arbitrary to the logical. Problems of motivation are decreased when there is a shared understanding of the decision framework. The planning process provides the decision framework.

One of the most challenging tasks for a CFO is to link plans to the budgeting process. The following is a special section that explores this challenge. The focus of the section is on the preparation necessary to bring about a successful link between the two processes.

Special Section

LINKING PLANNING AND BUDGETING: ARE YOU READY?

Linking strategic planning ideas and budgeting can be as easy as buttoning a shirt or as hard as buttoning a shirt with neither buttons nor buttonholes. If our efforts at planning have coasted along with no thought to budgets, and if budgets have always been made with no reflection of plans, then linking them is going to be challenging indeed.

Although planning and budgeting can be linked specifically, the two things are, in fact, metaphors for larger categories of activities. Planning is the set of activities that organizational members engage in to comprehend, prepare for, and challenge the future. Our day-to-day activities rarely bring the future into focus. Our heads are down, and we are banging away. Emergencies, quick decisions, hiring choices, and resource allocations all go bang, bang, bang. Budgeting is a metaphor for all those activities we do day to day. Budgets are the manifestation of resource-allocation decisions. Parallel with budgets, but as part of the same management process, we also hire and fire, we set policies and procedures, and we give reasons why we do what we do. Most budgeting cycles include setting policies and targets for hiring, tuition, and salary increases. Besides the numbers, we usually prepare a document explaining and justifying the budget. The integration of all these management activities is the budget process.

Linking strategic thought and budgeting thus means bringing day-to-day decisions, especially resource allocations, in line with the university's intended direction. Strategic planning is very much about direction. It points to goals in the future and paths to get there. Imagine an institution picking its way along a path marked with pitfalls, competitors nipping at institutional heels, and sudden landslides blocking the way. Strategic thinking is about knowing the way; budgeting says what we have to do *today* to move in that direction.

As in all things, preparation is everything. We can pinch two lapels of a buttonless shirt together, but when we let go, they fall apart. Planners must be mindful that their work will influence budgets. Budgeters must recognize that they are responsible for the success of strategies. Organizations must be prepared to button the present to the future.

What follows are a series of questions not far from "Do you have buttons?" and "Do you have thread?" While asking about your readiness, these questions also offer hints on ways to get ready to link strategic thinking to budgeting.

Is your budget ready for linking? Budgeting has a long and successful history. (See LeLoup [1988] for a description and history of microbudgeting [incrementalism] and macrobudgeting [goal-directed budgeting].) Budgeting processes differ greatly in levels of participation, amount of central decision-making, and incentive and reward structures (Dickmeyer, 1992, 246–54). As we become more mindful of the connections that can fruitfully occur between strategic thinking and budgeting, we see opportunities to improve both. The first area of opportunity is budget reporting.

1. **Can you produce reports structured to show the resources spent on plan initiatives?** Strategic plans generally present a series of initiatives that are important if the institution is to meet its goals. As discussed above, these are given as a series of primary principles. Strategic plans should confirm what is important and what is not. Most strategic plans give a series of challenges, initiatives, or focus areas that must be addressed to assure success in the future. These give the institution direction, and they focus institutional efforts.

    Unfortunately, these principles or initiatives rarely line up with budget reporting systems. Budgets focus on responsibility and present revenues and expenditures in the same fashion that accounting systems record the information. While a plan might point out the importance of improving undergraduate education, budget reports can only tell you what was spent on faculty salaries in English and history. Budget reports generally do not show the resources, and certainly not the *new* resources, put toward the strategy to improve undergraduate teaching efforts in the departments of English and history. This hinders the use of budgets to demonstrate planning results. As Joseph White (1988) points out, "the budget process records but does not set priorities."

    Even more challenging would be reporting from budget data on an initiative, for example, to improve retention. New resources for this effort could be budgeted in instruction, instructional support, student services, athletics, auxiliary enterprises, scholarships, and even plant maintenance. Extracting, benchmarking, watching trends, and measuring effectiveness with the deployment of these additional resources confounds standard budget reporting.

Budget directors who wait until the request comes down for a report of budget expenditures by plan initiative are likely to be frustrated. Several avenues of preparation are possible.

a. Some institutions can harness the power of the coding already available in their chart of accounts and current reporting system. For example, some institutions may have digits in the account code structure for an unused or poorly used level of reporting. Single campus institutions may run accounting systems that have code space for "location." The location code can be used, for example, as the "Planning Initiative" code. Payroll entries and invoices could be coded to include the initiative for which the work is dedicated. This does increase the work of the accounting staff, and it calls for higher levels of judgment as they examine the coding given on expenditures. Nevertheless, accounting packages that have these unused coding levels can produce reports based on these structures with limited manual intervention.

b. Other institutions may already pack their codes with information and may not wish to purchase a more robust accounting package. These institutions may choose to maintain a parallel database of expenditures coded by initiative. The database may be populated automatically from expenditure reports for a portion of expenditures using a crosswalk table. This is possible when expenditures from one category all count toward one initiative. In many cases, however, this will not be possible. Recording the expenditures by initiative in the database becomes entirely manual at this point. All expenditures for new laboratory equipment may automatically be coded for the renovated science lab initiative, but not all financial aid expenditures may go toward the retention initiative.

In general, departments would have to note the initiative to be charged, along with the usual accounting information. Then a new position in accounting (undoubtedly) would have to manually post to the database the charge for the initiative. The database would then provide the reports.

Institutions may find it easier to take a statistical sample of expenditures by area and estimate expenditures on an annual basis.

c.   The final method relies on department managers to estimate the proportion of their area's expenditures each month that are dedicated to various initiatives. While this method results in approximate numbers only, manager involvement in allocating resources to initiatives is increased. This increased attention to resource allocations toward initiatives could foster greater attention to initiative success.

2.   **Can you produce reports that show revenue improvements from various initiatives?** This is not a quick-answer question. The most likely revenue-enhancement initiative is of the "improve fund-raising results" type. While the budgeting system has always set targets and budgets for gift funds, the questions become: What counts? And, is the payoff from the increase in resources to this initiative sufficient?

The true aim of many initiatives is revenue enhancement. Better revenue streams from research projects, inventions, intellectual property, and business incubators are occasionally targeted. Stronger tuition revenue streams should result from broadened markets, from new academic concentrations in areas of greater demand and from improved retention. Budget reports give revenues by source, but can they also show revenue change resulting from strategic initiatives?

When budget directors try to link financial results to revenue enhancement planning goals, the planners realize that the goals can and must be quantified in terms of available data.

a.   Fund-raising goals can be stated in terms of dollars raised per dollar of funds invested, usually over several years to capture the delayed effect of investments ("cultivation"). It is important to stipulate what kinds of funds are to be included in the goal (alumni or corporate, unrestricted or restricted). It is also important to define what categories of costs are to be included as investments (telethons and/or annual reports). Planners need to decide if they want to maintain their return from investment, or set a better return as their goal.

b. Revenue improvements in many special areas, like research and patent royalties, are usually measured well in accounting systems. The challenge comes when the revenues come with cost-sharing provisions. Research projects that do not generate full coverage of overhead may be shifting the general support burden to other revenue sources.

c. Tuition revenues can be shown as generated from a number of initiative-related sources. By dividing annual tuition and fee revenue by a full year of enrollment full-time equivalents (FTEs), a budget director can find the *average revenue per FTE per enrollment period*. Institutions may also compute average year-to-year retention and average new enrollment levels as percentages of the previous fall's FTE enrollment. An *expected number of returning students* can thus be computed using the average retention rate, and the *variance in the number of returning students* can also be computed by subtracting the average retention rate from the actual rate and multiplying by the base number of students available for retention (usually total previous enrollment minus graduating students). The *expected number of students* can be computed using the previous fall's enrollment times the average proportion of new students to enrollment, and the *variance in the number of new students* can be found by subtracting the average percentage of new students of the previous fall's number from the actual percentage and multiplying by the previous fall's number.

Tuition revenue can thus be attributed to four pieces of the enrollment pie: the expected number of returning students, the expected number of new students, the variance number of returning students, and the variance number of new students. The two variances can be used to describe the revenue success of retention and recruitment initiatives by multiplying the FTE enrollment numbers of each by the average tuition revenue per FTE mentioned above. These kinds of hard metrics too often are not forthcoming from budgeting and accounting staff. They are not all that difficult.

3. **Can you generate cost/benefit analyses for any strategic recommendation?** This question pushes further than just reporting on the financial consequences of initiatives. It asks whether budget offices are ready to be involved in the evaluation of potential plan initiatives. Does the budget office have the analytic power to assist directly in the strategic planning process?

   a. Does the budget office have databases with expense and revenue data that can be easily manipulated to sort costs into new categories?

   b. Can the budget office abandon the "count every penny" accounting mentality and use sampling techniques (like auditors do) to estimate probable expenses, when a pile of manual work might normally be required?

   c. Can the budget office develop techniques to find the true marginal costs and revenues associated with initiatives, including surveys of budget officers asking what expenses would go up if we undertook this initiative?

   d. Can the budget office produce fact-based cost and revenue studies for a proposed initiative quickly? In this way initiatives can be shaped to have reasonable financial goals that can be measured within the budget system.

4. **Do all budget proposals within the budget process require justification in terms of plan principles, initiatives, and priorities?** There is considerable potential for using zero-based budgeting (ZBB) techniques to better link budgets and plans (For more on ZBB, see Meisinger, 1994, 181–82, and LeLoup, 1988, 29). Zero-based budgeting rests on the premise that everything, including continuing funding levels, must be justified. A strategic direction should provide the framework for justification. The key allowable justification is that the budget requested supports an activity that is in line with a strategic initiative or with several initiatives. How will this requested faculty position help improve undergraduate education? Will this requested financial aid office position help improve retention?

Resource allocation decisions require trade-offs—choosing among alternatives to find the most effective and efficient means of moving the institution toward its goals. This requires not only that budget requests be justified in conceptual terms as working within an initiative, but also that the requests provide analyses that demonstrate that each provides the best method for doing so.

Suppose we are at a university that must restrict enrollment growth because of limited classroom availability. Suppose also, however, that it has developed a strategic principle to serve more people, and this requires an increase in enrollment. Then suppose that the business staff develop an opportunity to replace all the university's copy shop equipment and save 8 percent on copying costs or about $200,000. The university could also, however, outsource its copying with no savings, but it could easily recycle the space as a 20-person classroom. The replacement of the copy equipment probably could not fit into any existing principle, other than, perhaps, better service. Let's do some calculations on this situation. One new classroom means that about 16 more courses could be offered each semester in the space or 32 in an academic year. A full-time equivalent student takes six courses per year. So, 32 courses with 20 students divided by 6 means that one new classroom could enable about 107 new FTE enrollments a year. For this institution let us assume that each FTE student nets $8,000 after scholarships and the marginal costs of recruiting, utilities, instruction, and instructional support. Outsourcing copying could thus improve net revenue annually by $856,000! This figure, of course, needs to be diminished by the risks that 107 more students would not come and thus, that each new class would not be full. Given low levels of these risks, it looks like we can make this budget judgment in strategic terms. The loss of savings is well outweighed by the gain in revenues from the new space.

Is Your Strategic Plan Ready to Be Linked? The burden of preparation for linking does not fall entirely on the budgeting system. Vague plans that are "hard to pin down" and that lack measurable goals or strict financial constraints make the effort of linking to budgets extremely difficult (Tuckman and Chang, 1990, 73–74). Budgets are meant to be hard and concrete. Budgets are tough tools for the management of expectations. Budgets say, "Do it with this and no more!" Plans that are little more than abstract exhortations to excellence—comfort words for the insiders—cannot be linked to budgets. Velcro doesn't cling to buttons. Addressing the following questions when preparing the institution to begin strategic planning can greatly ease the linking effort.

1. **Is the plan broad enough to encompass all aspects of the institution?** Is every office able to evaluate its use of resources in terms of the priorities set by the plan? One of the marks of a linkable plan is that it assists the entire institution in setting course. All members of the university community should feel that the strategic plan defines for them those activities that are most important and the ways of pursuing those activities that would be most beneficial for moving the institution toward its goals.

Today's budgets cover the entire organization, not just favored aspects. Every member of the community works within budget expenditure constraints, revenue targets, and special incentives. If the planning effort does not result in answers to questions as mundane as why we have custodians or security officers and what excellent custodial service and security is, then the plan becomes partially irrelevant to the budget.

After defining the goals, values, and strategic approaches, the vice president for administration should be able to ask, "Given these values, strategic approaches and principles, Ms. Director of Security, what should be the values, strategic direction, and principles of your operation and what must you be doing to help the institution reach its vision?" If the director of security is only able to say, "I'm not sure what "excellence in education," "valuing the discovery of knowledge," and "a university for the best" mean to my department, then the outcomes of the planning process have probably been too abstract to have any meaning for day-to-day operations. The director of security may have difficulty justifying another security post in terms of "excellence in education."

2. **Does the plan spell out what "success" would look like in enough detail to allow measurement of progress?** This question is another look at the problem of abstract plans, specifically the often-abstract definition of success. Plans should present a vision with principles that make success measurable. The vision should picture the institution reaching success in the future. Some golf holes cannot be seen from the tee. Yet, to be successful, the golfer must know the direction and see with his or her mind's eye the invisible target. The golfer must also visualize the traps, the water hazards, and the rough. Until we can picture these things through appropriate practice and reconnaissance, we may as well just smash the ball any old way and hope for the best.

"Affordability" may be a goal that implies a particular combination of strategies of frugality, financial aid, and tuition pricing. To link this concept to budgeting and reporting, however, requires a more precise idea of what the goal is and how it is defined (Schaffer, 1992, 83). A more precise definition would narrow the goal to the particular sector of society that the institution had most successfully served, perhaps the second-quartile income group. The goal might be that net tuition for this group should not exceed some percentage of family income. Without agreement on this definition, the budget process cannot relate expenditure targets, financial aid strategies, and tuition pricing policies to the plan. Too often the link is so tenuous that a budgeted tuition increase can only be accompanied by the statement, "Tuition has been increased by 5 percent, a figure slightly higher than our hopes for the coming year."

3. **Does the plan suggest what activities are the most critical for moving the institution toward success?** Does the plan go beyond a vision? Does the plan note roadblocks along the path to the vision? Does the plan note where the institution has developed the greatest strengths that can help it rise above its competitors? New funding or additional funding should only be justified in terms of critical priorities. Most institutions have done a rather good job of linking plans and budgets at this point. New or additional funding justifications rest on the critical initiatives listed in the plan.

Nevertheless, some plans appear to flow, not from strategic priorities, but from the project lists themselves. That is, administrators develop a "most wanted" list of projects—nice things to have (and some are indeed critical)—and then draw up the list of "planning initiatives" to fit. The flow to institutional strategies for success is dubious. While the linking is successful, because we started with the project budgets and produced a plan to fit, the plan is not. The plan will appear arbitrary and contrived to those seeking to understand the allocation of resources in the budget.

4. **Does the plan suggest what activities are necessary, but not critical, for moving the institution toward success?** Level funding justifications must rest on more than just the limits of resources. Offices should know that their necessary, but not critical, efforts must be maintained, but that *new* investment in these functions is not viewed as critical to the institution's reaching its vision.

A plan with the theme "everything is wonderful" will be difficult to link to budgets. Too seldom a plan actually goes beyond the "uplifting." To be useful to the budgeting process a plan must note not only what is critical for success, but also what must be maintained for success.

Having the best, most modern, most efficient bursar's office in the world may be a wonderful thing, but it might be absolutely meaningless in terms of the success of the institution. Having a bursar's office that addresses the strategies of the institution and does not fail on any of its critical functions may be a more appropriate goal for that office and for its budget.

5. **Does the plan suggest what activities are not necessary to move the institution toward success?** Many plans address this question through omission, but often it is hard to tell activities that should be discarded from those that should be merely maintained. Budgets are the vehicle through which reductions are announced. Plans that lack criteria for culling activities leave the budget hanging by a thread unworthy of being called a link.

What are the criteria for outsourcing the bookstore or any administrative activity? What are the criteria for continuing a department? Should departments with no students and few service courses be continued? What are the justifications for a reduction of support? Institutions that refuse to burden planning with these difficult and very political questions should not expect an easy time linking plans to budgets. Fortunately, budgeting processes are continually being revised to make it more possible for these decisions to be made. The new processes show more clearly how resources are generated and give more and more responsibility to those who generate the resources to make the more difficult decisions. Nevertheless, if the planning process does not foster tough decisions, then planning and budgets will not be well linked.

6. **Does the plan list values and ethics that describe initiatives and behaviors that will be shunned and not given support?** One area our budgeting solutions have not developed well is resource allocation decisions specifically justified on value or ethical considerations. A robust planning process can unearth and vivify values that can have a major impact on the budget.

The best example comes from the Ivy League, where some institutions have declared that undergraduates should not have to graduate with excessive loan burdens. This is both a value and a competitive consideration, and it certainly has affected the budgets of these institutions. Endowment spending is being diverted from general support to student financial aid, limiting activity expense growth somewhat. While the assertion of this value may not have come explicitly from a strategic planning process, it is an excellent example of a strategic change fostered by a value.

7. **Does the plan describe methods of searching for opportunities in ways that allow for new budgets?** A good strategic process must do more than say, "These things are good." It must not cut off creativity and the search for opportunities. It should define what an opportunity might look like and endorse the investment in resources in such activities.

Effective budgeting uses reallocation disciplines to set aside resources for the unexpected, both good and bad. Planning can help define for the organization what a legitimate opportunity is. Budgeting can provide the flexibility to fund the investment. Has the strategic process, for example, provided ground rules for evaluating whether an idea of distance education or a major in GPS marketing would be a worthwhile investment? What evidence should be presented? What justifications are needed? In what directions should faculty and staff entrepreneurs be encouraged to look? What incentives are available to encourage an entrepreneurial spirit?

The planning process can be a source of ideas of directions, criteria, and necessary justifications. The budgeting process should allow the "idea people" to present their plans, within the strategic framework of directions and justifications. The budgeting process is still where the resource allocation decisions are made. The planning process needs to be pushed to develop the rules.

8. **Is the planning process efficient and dynamic enough to regularly feed new ideas into the budgeting process?** This question goes beyond the previous question. Question 7 was aimed at shaping one of the outcomes of planning: encouragement of the search for opportunities. This question aims at the dynamics of the planning process.

The search for opportunities should not follow last year's rules. New opportunities can be suggested by current successes. A plan cannot be five years in the making and put up on a shelf. A plan must be a dynamic process of observation, communication, and assessment (Dunn, et al., 1992, 63–65). If 1997 was the year of opportunities, what is 2004? How many universities still have their best strategic thinking locked in a 1998 document called A Plan for the 21st Century?

Thus, the planning process itself must not be a burden but a part of every day's activities. It must contain a continual search for opportunities and a continual questioning of principles, values, and strategies. It must interact with day-to-day decision making such that the budget process does not grow stale from year to year, searching for opportunities from the last decade.

IS YOUR ORGANIZATION READY FOR LINKING BUDGETS TO PLANS?

So now you've sewn on your buttons, and you've made the buttonholes, but wait, how dexterous are your fingers? While you may have the proper technology for linking budgets and plans, you may not be organizationally ready. The budget is the technology we use to *commit* an organization to the actions that were declared priorities in the plan. But for the link to really work, the organization has to be ready to accept these commitments.

1. **Is the leadership team willing to make choices and ratify ideas?** Lack of leadership can effectively derail the linking process. The planning process can provide great strategic ideas; the budget process can provide powerful tracking tools for the ideas. Nevertheless, it takes leadership to push the ideas into the budget.

   Someone has to connect the dots. Without leadership, budgeting will continue as it always has: accepting the past, pushing new ideas down to fit available resources, and lacking accountability for results. Having the technology is not the same thing as having the will. Although this seems obvious, too often this is where everything breaks down.

2. **Can anything, once started, be stopped? (Is there a culture of assessment? Is there courage?)** Strategic thinking is all about picking up an organization and facing it in a new direction. It is about priorities and focus. It is about feeding some areas, maintaining some areas, and stopping other areas. Budgets are more the evidence that some effort has been stopped than they are the methodology for stopping efforts. Some organizations have excluded "stopping" from their cultures.

   Many institutions have a "culture of defense," rather than a culture of assessment. "I can tell you 25 reasons why what I am doing is good," is the existing attitude, not "I can show you three measures that demonstrate that what I do has positive consequences for the institution, and, fortunately, they look good, but I think we can improve."

Changing the culture is not easy. Nevertheless, without a cultural shift, why plan? Change would be easier if

a.   People were involved in the decision to change.

b.   Retraining had a successful track record at the institution.

c.   The changes were understood to be part of a strategic framework (Lahey, 2003, 8).

d.   Change itself was promoted as part of a healthy organization.

e.   The organization was actually better off after the change, as shown by measures understood before the change.

3.   **Has learning been institutionalized?** At too many places, forgetting seems to be what has been institutionalized. Are there people who assist members of the institution in remembering how things "used to be" (that is, the awful way things used to be)?

Plans that year after year have the same core of impossible projects come out of organizations that forget why they never started these projects. Why start a curriculum with no interested students? Why build a dormitory that cannot be financed? Are these solutions looking for problems? Could they be implemented if creatively rethought? Learning requires that we admit that we have something to learn.

Budgets that only incrementally adjust from year to year are another form of evidence that the organization does not value learning. Unless the budget process demonstrates reflection about what is working and what is not, it cannot be used as part of the implementation methodology for the best plans.

4.   **Has your organization found a way to generate the face-to-face communications of meetings without the productivity-killing time demands and the logistical constraints of real meetings?** Organizations are turning to asynchronous distance learning to assist learners whose schedules and lives do not allow classroom learning. I have seen universities where 70 percent of the distance learners are also enrolled in classroom-based courses. Why? Because between work, home, and family, that second or third course can only be done at midnight or on Sunday. Staff and faculty face the same challenges. Meetings, like classes, must commence at the appointed hour. Not

only that, but oral communication, while wonderfully nuanced, is terribly inefficient.

By using asynchronous distance-learning technology, meetings can be conducted all week long, at the leisure of the participants. Streaming conversations can be monitored and steered by committee chair editors. Diversions can be put in their own streams. Participants can add comments, attach articles, and add graphs online.

Online meeting has several advantages. Planning means looking ahead further than today's emergencies. By using a different modality to conduct this business, the sense of separation from each day's demands can be enhanced. The asynchronous modality can also be used to increase participation. Most committees stop functioning efficiently above seven members. Asynchronous classrooms seem to be fairly manageable at around 20.

Institutions must use available technology to make planning and consultation less of a burden than it currently is.

5. **Is everything on the table?** An interesting question to ask before an institution begins planning and then attempting to link the plans to the budgets is the "sacred cow" question. Can we consider outsourcing? Can we consider retraining? Can we look for new student markets? Can we consider new technologies for learning and administration? Attempting to do something that is taboo, especially something that is taboo to the leadership, will kill any attempt to link planning and budgeting. The number of taboo areas needs to be limited and clearly defined.

So, are you ready to link planning and budgeting? Do you have the right technologies, methodologies, and cultures? If so, linking is easy. If not, then you probably have several years of preparation ahead of you. Fear not, however. Carefully preparation that addresses each question above, slowly changing each answer from "no" to "yes," will make linking budgets to plans as easy as buttoning your shirt.

A Day in the Life: Marnie Strathy, CFO, Vichy Community College

As Vice President Strathy drove toward campus early one Wednesday in late April, she noticed that the neighborhoods near campus had become sheathed in the brilliant lavender of Redbuds that had bloomed seemingly overnight. "The early bloom catches the warming bee," she mused, delighted at having originated a poetic saying so early in the day. She then thought of the opportunities and challenges faced by the tree of her life, Vichy Community College.

She liked thinking in threes: three new opportunities, three new obstacles, and three new strategies. The opportunities came from the need of VCC's region for teachers and nurses and the need for many of the region's returning military personnel to slide back into successful civilian life. The obstacles came from new for-profit, distance-education schools offering relatively inexpensive programs in low-cost, high-margin academic areas, from a stagnant economy, from slowing job creation and county support, and from aging facilities.

The strategies had come largely from discussion with the president and other vice presidents. They had realized that isolation was no longer working and that they needed partnerships to help provide teachers and nurses and to sharpen vets' training for the few non-teaching and non-nursing jobs becoming available. They knew that a strategic alliance with various armed forces agencies to provide more than just "classes for vets" was going to be an important direction for them. They also knew that, because of the size of their service area and the schedules of people, sometimes working several jobs and keeping a home, they had to move their services from campus buildings to the Internet. She had thought of the slogan for this new emphasis: "Reach out, build bridges, build lives."

When Marnie reached her office, she dug into her e-mail. She put aside items with longer attachments to read later in the day. A morning person, she didn't like to waste her creative energy with low-energy tasks like absorbing the thoughts of others. She sat on several virtual committees, and Wednesday morning was usually her time to update her contributions. Her role in the environment committee was to track price and market share positions. She had fostered a relationship with several other CFOs in institutions that often sought to attract the same students and had convinced them that as long as they didn't make any joint financial decisions, sharing data would benefit them all. As a result, she provided her committee, and eventually the campus, with pie charts on enrollment and first-year student market shares, sticker-price position, and net price position (after grant aid). April marked the time when many colleges were making tuition decisions, so she was updating her charts and preparing to share them with the committee.

She also realized that it was her responsibility to interpret the new information. One of the cautions she noted was that one of the proprietary schools offering online bachelor's degree completion for nurses was showing a large national increase in enrollments and had announced no increase in tuition for next year. She had used her contacts at area hospitals to gauge competitive enrollments and realized that the online program was becoming increasingly popular in VCC's region.

When she went to the environment committee's Web site, she found several other postings from others having scanning responsibilities. She saw that the director of financial aid had filed a projection of the impact of new federal financial aid regulations and that the registrar had posted an update on veterans' benefits. There also was a series of product reviews by the director of distance education.

She checked into the vision committee's Web site and noticed that there had been no changes or even suggestions posted in the last week. The online activity of that group had peaked in February, when they had taken the president's list of 57 things beginning with "I see a college in 2010 that . . ." and cut, combined, and reworded it to a list of nine vision elements. The first thing to go had been number 27: "I see a college in 2010 that has a statue of me in the quad."

She had decided that she would finish the pricing plan for the year after next in May, but she had gained a fairly strong consensus with the pricing team. Two years ago the state had allowed each community college district to set its own tuitions within very strict boundaries. The pricing plan, however, included tuition decisions for special programs and not-for-credit activities. Fee decisions were included, as were decisions about the parameters for the need-based student financial aid funding formula. Finally, decisions about discounts for particular groups, partnership members, and special situations were included.

The plan also contained position statements to academic partners on tuition prices for programs that represented continuations of VCC initial programs. She had championed the idea that their mission of service to the people of their region dictated that pricing was the "lead-off" strategy. VCC had to price its programs, and she included the price of the continuation program offered by VCC partners in this concept, such that VCC's services were broadly available and such that they satisfied the region's needs. Resources were more likely to follow successful service presentation. The challenge, as always, was to find ways to provide the services within the limits of the revenue raised.

Integrating the pricing strategy with knowledge of the environment and with program and service strategies was a skill of which she was proud. For example, she had pointed out that the people they served had incomes that were more homogeneous and lower than the general population and of many other institutions. With this in mind, it made little strategic sense to run tuitions up while supporting more needy students with financial aid, since a large majority of students were all equally needy. It was best to price at a level that this lower-income, "bread and butter" student could afford and minimize institutional financial aid that normally allowed "price discrimination" based on income.

Not all programs served the same clientele, however. They had partnered with a nearby four-year college to provide an online bachelor's degree completion program for working adults. Costs were higher, but the ability to pay was also somewhat higher for this group. The partner had been particularly interested, however, in providing a competitively lower-cost program by having VCC provide any necessary lower-division courses to the students in the program. The cost to degree for these students taking a combination of courses from both colleges was cheaper than from competitors, and VCC was able to get seed money from the state to assist in the development of online course technology that could also be used to develop courses for students not interested in the program. This improved VCC's overall cost effectiveness.

She was particularly proud of how quickly she helped get VCC through the teacher shortage crisis.

The strategic orientation she had helped design for VCC called for out-of-the-box thinking to solve the region's problems. For many years, they had anticipated that the state would build a four-year university in the county. Plans were drawn up. The current state fiscal crisis, however, had put the plans on hold indefinitely. Meanwhile, the demand for teachers increased at a rate that could not be satisfied by the small, private colleges in the area. More and more VCC graduates were turning to for-profit, online universities to prepare for teaching. Nevertheless, state education authorities were hesitant about the level of preparation of online graduates and put up many roadblocks.

Their mission highlighted the opportunity. Their strength was lower-division instruction. They also had strong relationships with area schools and the state education department. The strategy called for building partnerships. A team of faculty members evaluated online education programs and found two they thought met quality standards. After a short series of discussions, the team chose to work with a for-profit university because of its willingness to tailor a program to the area's needs while satisfying the quality criteria of the state board of education.

An online task force was formed with representatives from area schools, the proprietary school's education department, the state education department, and VCC. The result was a unique program, where the first two years of coursework were provided at VCC. The task force developed the courses, and the proprietary school guaranteed 100 percent transfer of all courses with grades of C or above. In turn, the area schools developed student teacher opportunities for students in the program. The for-profit school guaranteed that no student would be allowed to graduate without passing the state's certification exams. The for-profit also agreed to share with VCC its understanding of the technology of online course development. This meant that VCC could expand online offerings with less investment and more success, thus relieving some of the strain on brick and mortar infrastructure.

She sat at her desk and thought, "What three new opportunities did I see yesterday?"

Seven Key Thoughts

1. Shaping a more strategic attitude is background; action is foreground. The institution's guidance system should be set to operate in the background. Decisions and action are the here and now. Planning should not be another scene, separate from work life. It must be the background of work life.

2. The strategic attitude requires daily sight in many directions:
   a. Begin with looking around (environmental scanning);
   b. Then look inside (capabilities, strengths, weaknesses);
   c. Then look back (have we moved?); and
   d. Look ahead (do I clearly know where we are going?). I have emphasized the relationship between planning and looking. Strategic planning is the formalized set of activities that requires a person to pick his or her head up from the desk and from the office and to look around at the world at trends and at one's own organization as a whole. One must look for trends in the world around, finding a place in the future that fits. One must look for trends within the organization and find there the evidence for strengths and weaknesses.

3. Choices, like those found in budget decisions, define foreground activities. What must be evident from strategic thought to assist in making budget decisions (or personnel decisions or site decisions)? Choices result in actions and influence. Actions and influence determine the direction of change within an organization. The choices among alternatives are always made within a framework. The more the framework is uniform among organizational participants, the more quickly the organization will be able to move in the chosen direction.

4. Evidence of successful linking between background (planning) and foreground (action) comes when each element of the budget can be shown to make sense in the context of the strategic direction of the university. A plan is more than a book of sweet words. It presents the framework that makes sense of the choices.

5. Actions, for example, budget elements, cannot all fit within the university's strategic context, when a plan is reduced to a list of projects. Projects should not be allowed to drive strategies. Strategies must come from a more abstract look at the world around and the world within. Too often organizations become burdened with "solutions":

the things that competitors do; the great ideas that we read. When solutions drive the goals, the goals become trivial.

6. A healthy organization has many opportunities for nontraditional, but important, roles, like "The Values Czar," "The Chief Learning Officer," and "The Strategy Maven." Universities have always deeply valued the brilliant statement and the status of traditional, respected roles. Unfortunately, a pathology has developed where the brilliant statement has replaced the idea that is good for the group as a whole, and grasping for respect has replaced respect for the full range of possible roles that are necessary for success.

7. Technology now allows us to interact on our own schedule. Monitoring the environment, such as changes in pricing, programs, or image among competitors; regulatory changes; and employment opportunities for graduates can be narrowly assigned to task force members with individual contributions simply made to an e-mail list. The death of the university as we know it—as a community, not just an organization; as participants shaping a joint future, not just passive workers—comes from strangulation by committee. Technology, for once, may save us by giving us strong connections to each other with greater flexibility in time and by giving us greater control over irrelevance.

Chapter Twelve
THE ROLE OF LEADERSHIP

Establishing a strategic organization presents leaders of the organization with serious challenges. Taking away the planning project deprives leadership of one of the most direct ways of giving direction to the organization—leadership by project advancement. Integrating planning and operating increases the responsibility of leadership to infuse the organization as a whole with direction and values.

With the project-list style of planning, the main role of the president is to make sure that his or her favorite projects get on the list and get implemented. These lists also demonstrate the imprint of the provost and the CFO. Each makes his or her mark on the university by completing big, important projects, and he or she with the most projects completed wins. Shaping the university one project at a time leaves a tangible record of each leader. Afterward, people can point to a collection of buildings, majors, or financial systems as being the legacy of a particular regime.

The critical questions under this strategic organization methodology remain the same: "When do I step in and when do I step back?" "When do I guide and when do I decide?" "When do I energize and when do I deny?"

Is this a village or an organization? Am I the mayor or a CEO? The answer, of course, is a little of both. Constituencies are powerful, able by majority vote to undo an administration's wishes. Laws constrain, while presidential injunctions are sometimes ignored. Conversely, administrations are not without power. People can be fired for insubordination, and the administration really does decide pay rates. Although the academic side of the house is more like a village (with limited enfranchisement for certain populations, like part-time faculty) and administrative responsibilities are exercised with corporate ideals in mind, the two models are neither perfect nor well separated (Green, 1988a, 17).

The trick is to know what a successful mayor knows about running a corporation and what a CEO knows about being successful in politics. Assert your rights for what is yours, listen carefully and with humility, and make sure those with other responsibilities take them seriously. It is a fallacy to assume that, like a mayor, all power rests with the acquiescence of the people. It is also a fallacy to believe that, like a CEO, the administration has all power.

The role of the president and his or her administration is thus defined by a series of responsibilities within the strategic framework. In some cases the responsibility is heavy, requiring decision and forcefulness. In others, a guiding hand is more appropriate. Although personal leadership style can shade these suggestions, there are certainly many styles that would be incompatible with this version of strategic direction.

Affirm the mission. The mission is wholly the responsibility of the president. While the board is the ratifying body, only the president and his or her administration can bring to bear the arguments that compel the board's decision. Not only must the president say, "Yes, that's it," but he or she must also repeat before all audiences, "This is our mission. . . . These people are the people that we serve. . . . This is why we exist. . . . This is what makes us special." Chait (1992, 35) also urges the board to lead the celebration of a mission.

While leading the charge, the president still must quietly be able to say, "But I could be wrong. Times change, you know" (Gardiner, 1988, 149). The president needs to entertain a dialog, without entertaining the ideas, until they are fully supported and obvious. Every idea must be met with more questions. Every idea must be challenged to stand up to the thoughts of others, especially board members. The president should not waiver from support of the current mission, except to support dialogue, until a new idea's time has come. The need to mix devotion to mission and responsiveness is well developed in Hornstein's *Managerial Courage* (1986, 181).

Ask about the future. Leaders ask about the future. We do this because each point of view has an element of probability to it, and because we want everyone to be thinking about the implications for what we see now. Conjuring up a vision requires sharing views of the future. Inductive processes are fueled from the combustion of multiple theories—each theory challenging the last or each theory adding another element of truth.

Theories do not die easily. They are challenged by the facts that are daily discovered, if these facts are not ignored because they challenge the reigning theory (Kuhn, 1962). It is only a theory that partnerships will strengthen the institution. The theory is challenged when the local hospital will join in a partnership with the college to broaden nurses' education only if tuition is waived. We must modify the theory because we learn that partnerships for the sake of partnerships can weaken the university.

Leaders asking about the future are part of the discipline of strategic thinking. The future is important. Tomorrow is created by the things we (and others) do today. The leader asks, "That's a lovely idea, but what effect will it have on the university in five years? Put on your political science hat. What will be the political fallout? Put on your anthropologist's hat. How will the culture respond or change? Put on your economist's hat. What incentives to behavior does this change produce? How does all this change the big picture of the university? Is this good?"

Proclaim the vision. The vision belongs to the president and the administration. Ideally, a broad base of people on campus will endorse it, but it must be seen as unhesitatingly favored by the administration. The president must proclaim the vision almost as often as he or she proclaims the mission. Doubts and disagreements among administrators must be put aside everywhere beyond the closed doors of the president's cabinet.

The university vision requires personal commitment. The president talks about what he or she sees in the future of the institution. The administration takes full responsibility for getting the university there. The vision must be seen as very difficult, even a little impractical, the president's slightly crazy idea, but something worth trying for. That's the leadership part. The vision is not just stated; it belongs to a worthy person. Fulfilling the vision is done for the university and for the president. That is, the CEO cannot just order the university to go to the future of the vision. The university must trust the judgment of the president enough to say, "If Mary thinks we can get there and it will be better, then I will give it a shot" (Green, 1988a, 15). Much progress can be made in the development of trust if the president can establish the integrity of the vision with the mission and can demonstrate that the strengths of the university can be built on to get there.

If the vision is not connected to the mission in a tangible manner, or if the vision seems to be built from fragments that do not resemble current institutional strengths, then the administration will begin to lose trust. This is a failure of leadership.

Reinforce the values. While the president and administration have some control over values and can invent a few, values are usually heavily imbedded in the folklore and customs of the faculty, staff, and even students. This is especially true of the "old-time" faculty. There must be a process that puts words to the values, but it need not be controlled or even overseen by the president and administration. The president must be comfortable with the values and endorse them. He or she also needs to make sure that no important values have been left behind.

Trust is built when the president is able to say, "These are the university's values, and they are mine." We can hope that the presidential selection process has found a person comfortable with the institution's values. A service-oriented university selecting a dedicated researcher to be president would probably see increased conflict.

If the president has a personal, but relevant, value that does not come out of the values clarification process, the president should not hesitate to bring it out. The president may say, "I heartily accept these values and would like the community to consider the addition of this one. I feel strongly about it." Most of the work on values, however, comes in developing a statement that is unique to the university. "Dedication to learning" is fine, but it is meaningless in terms of the special values of the institution. "Dedication to learning in Lamoix County for people of all ages" sets out a new challenge.

Demand and support strategies. Realizing that there are big and little strategies, the president and his or her administration needs to take responsibility for only the three-to-six major strategies that define the direction of the institution. All other strategies need to be reviewed for consistency, but they do not require the visibility of the primary strategies.

Somewhat more than items in the vision, primary strategies require specialist thinking and focus. Still, each primary strategy requires that the administration be willing to commit a major amount of resources to their fulfillment. More than any of the other higher-level categories, strategies require accountability. The administration must be able to demonstrate that it fully supports each and has dedicated significant resources to them all. A call to improve retention with no identifiable support is empty rhetoric. Empty rhetoric erodes trust.

Push the principles. Because of their importance as integrators, those in the administration need to be seen as the primary force behind the principles. Also because of their responsibility for vision and values, administrators must not hesitate to endorse and take ownership of principles. Taking ownership does not necessarily mean claiming primary authorship. It does mean, "If it's not on my list, then it's not a university principle." That is, the pathway for suggesting principles, debating their merits, and raising objections should always be open, but there is only one list.

A leader will use the process of building principles to pinpoint priorities. The leader says, "These are things that are really important. I don't support doing other things, although I don't mind if you want to tell me that you think something else is more important."

Learn the concepts. University leaders actively pursue organizational learning. The vice president for development cannot afford to ignore explanations of the workings of the endowment or the latest research on learning under a distance-learning modality. Leaders learn the concepts and become the main explicators of each one.

Challenge assumptions. One of the rigors of modeling a system is that all assumptions have to be made explicit. Because models are simplifications of reality, the modeler must make a large number of simplifying assumptions. This is a good discipline to have, because leaders must find the assumptions and challenge them. A good model, like a good theory, has the most plausible simplifications. A good model contains the assumptions that, for the piece of the system being examined, one must do the least harm to the critical functioning of the system under the model. A financial model to be used to examine tuition policies that assumes little variance in stock market returns is fine when the endowment provides support for only 1 or 2 percent of the expenses. The model is much less satisfactory when the endowment supports 20 percent of the expenses. The assumption would make the model unusable in the face of the question: "What happens to our tuition pricing after three years of a bear market?"

Every model, theory, and prediction is based on assumptions. The leader must tease these out. The leader must set the example of finding and exposing the assumptions. The assumption you don't see *will* hurt you.

Develop teams. The key to the entire strategic thought process is to have teams made up of people who reason in different ways. (See the excellent discussion of "thinking roles" in Bensimon and Neumann (1993); also, see Green (1988b) for a discussion on presidents as "team leaders.") A team made up entirely of gifted deductive thinkers is little better than a dictator's circle of "yes men." These teams are extremely effective at implementing whatever project is handed to them. Unfortunately, too often the project is the wrong one.

Teams need to be taught to value people who think differently. There is nothing more troubling to a group of convergent thinkers than a divergent thinker. They have their theory. They are going to pound it to death. What is this guy doing walking around asking, "Have you tried this? Did you think of this? Maybe we should do it this way?" The deductive thinkers say, "The guy's crazy and getting on our nerves."

Teams need analyzers and synthesizers. They need people who pick ideas into little pieces to show what the ideas comprise. Teams also need people who take little pieces and put them together to show what the big picture is.

Teams need to learn to value the least-valued member. All teams have a least-valued member by tautological definition. There is no escape. There is always someone who doesn't seem to pull his or her weight, who doesn't care about quality, or who has other priorities. Such a person needs to be viewed as the knot, holding the skein together. Untie the knot and someone else takes his or her place, and so on, until the whole team unravels. If the team can be made to commit to the person, the person then needs to understand the team's perceptions of him or her. The person needs to be able to tell the team his or her reaction to the perceptions and to give his or her perceptions of the team. In the end, some value must be traded. The team must be able to grant that the person at least gives perspective to their excesses of enthusiasm. The team must build a role for that person, even if it is only as the group's humorist. The person may always be the goat, but the goat keeps the horses from getting too skittish. If we are going to keep a team of horses, it's best to keep a goat in the barn too.

Teams need contrarians and ratifiers. There are people who can only think of the counterexample. Teams will jump off cliffs if someone didn't say, "Did you ever think about this?" Teams also need the quiet person, who only says, "I think we've got something that will work." People recognize that the arguments are over. One idea, so bloody and bruised that no one recognizes the champion, still stands. The ratifier just has to raise the idea's arm.

Teams need the humorous and the glum. The person who can show the irony in something, injects realism and makes the process a little more fun. The glum person keeps the team from concentrating only on having fun. (For a discussion of group roles like these, see Fisher [1974, 50–53].)

Teams need people who have great visual ideas and people who see best with words. A person who visualizes his or her thoughts can better see relationships between tangible ideas. A wordsmith helps the team communicate its ideas more precisely.

The best leaders are not necessarily those with the greatest ideas (Keohane, 1992, 42). The best leaders can be those who put together the best teams.

Feed the energy. Being in a position to feed the energy of people with good ideas is a test of the effectiveness of this type of strategic planning. A leader with a static written plan, ending in a list of projects, would have to go outside of the plan to support an idea that is, well, outside of the plan. A leader of an organization that is thinking strategically is more likely to find an energetic person or group with ideas that are in the strategic direction of the institution.

A leader has to be able to say, "That's a great idea and you seem to have a lot of energy for it. It is in line with our strategic direction. What can I do to get out of your way?"

Dragging people, kicking and screaming, into the number one priority does not work. Getting out of the way of people with energy toward an idea, if it fits in the strategic direction of the institution, does work. As Drucker (2001, 241) suggests, work for "impact rather than technique." Impact requires energy; technique is passive.

Not all energetic ideas are going to fit within the strategic direction. These ideas cannot be supported. Sometimes a leader does have to get in the way. Nevertheless, if the strategic directions are well defined and accepted, the likelihood of energy gathering around them is greater. The choice of projects, however, should be shaped by strategies and driven by the energy of someone wanting to be a champion.

The path is finest when the enthusiast, not the laggard, paves it. The good path is the goal.

Manage expectations. A leader, however, does manage peoples' expectations, especially the CFO (Morgan, 1979, 54). The university is not all things to all people. Resources are not limitless. Connecting two dots with a straight line that points upward does not mean that the next dot is optimistically foreordained.

"Managing" does not only mean curtailing. The word implies understanding, predicting, and affecting. Expectations should be based on a set of reasoned ideas. Energy in the direction of a strategic emphasis is more likely to receive support. Budget requests with strategic underpinnings are more likely as well to receive support.

Every action of a leader affects expectations. Leaders are able to rise above the scene of actions and to view the world as a web of changing expectations. Organizations are built on relationships. Relationships are built on expectations. Budgets are the most explicit form of expectation management. Every strategic statement is going to affect expectations. Leaders are vividly conscious of their effect on expectations and know that their predictions are not always correct.

Evaluate the past. The cycle of strategic thought includes an audit phase, where each of the other phases is scrutinized. As a segment in a cycle, evaluation is both an end and a beginning. A university leader keeps the cycle going by using evaluations as part of a continuous cycle of new beginnings. Pfeffer (1992, 263) warns that organizations seem to fear critically reviewing the past. The key is to put the past in the context of the future.

The focus must always be on the next project, the next registration, or the amended vision. We must ask, "What will we do differently the next time? Why?" The audit is not a time of finding blame or of wishing that things were different. The audit is part of the preparation for the future.

No project is complete without an evaluation. Sometimes projects wind down into a series of tiny, ongoing implementations. At this point an evaluation has to be "staged" to give some closure to a never-ending project. The chance to prepare for the future can be missed if no conclusion is made or recognized.

Audits can be institutionalized as celebrations. This is a good time to provide food, plaques, and party hats. The celebration should end with reflection: "What have we learned that will make the path smoother next time?" People should come to the celebration prepared to answer.

This is not to say that all faults can be forgiven. Audits are public events that celebrate risk taking and prepare the institution for the next set of risks. Evaluations are private. Failing to achieve the vision this year is forgivable. Failing to maintain core processes while pursuing the vision is not.

Celebrate. Do not just celebrate audits; celebrate to keep the organization focused on its own significance. One of the challenges of moving away from traditional strategic planning is that the focus moves from the end points to the path. It is much easier to celebrate reaching some end than it is to celebrate the walk on the path. Yet, the walk itself must be celebrated if people are to retain an understanding of the significance of the journey.

Goals define the direction, but the care taken on the journey gives meaning to existence. People should be rewarded for the care they take during the journey. The celebration of that care gives meaning and reinforces the idea of the path as the focus (Eckel and Kezar, 2003, 101).

Celebrations are public events where each person's significance is affirmed. Leaders are in the best position to affirm significance. The priest is the model. Priests have been powerful figures throughout history because they have understood the need for personal significance and the role of rituals in reinforcing significance.

Make up your own ritual. I like providing bagels and orange juice every last Friday of the month for each of my teams with an agenda of "What were last month's highlights? What's new for next month? What made us happy and what made us cry?" The leader says little other than, "Thank you for that. We needed that progress."

A Day in the Life: Eugene Romanowski, CFO, Sohmboll State University

Gene Romanowski sputtered to himself as he rifled the papers on his desk one Tuesday at 7:00 a.m., "One of these days I'm going to work for a president who sleeps. Ah, here it is." He put a final sheet in his briefcase and went up the back stairs of the administration building to the president's office. The president, who was already on the phone, motioned to him. "I think that's spectacular. Manny and I will be there, and thank you again for hooking Robinson. Getting the *Herald* to pay a little more attention to the good things at the university would be quite lovely. We'll see you next week. Bye."

"Good morning, Connie," Gene said, as Consuela Suarez, president of SSU, walked over to the conference table. "Do you think you can get Robinson to join 'The Circle of Friends'? He's one of the great invisible powers in the county."

Connie smiled, "Robinson went to school with Sam. I think we have a good chance with Sam as a bridge." Then her face turned glum, "Now, would you tell me what was going on at our last strategic planning steering committee meeting? After Barry got up and whined about being worn out trying to be all things to all people, the meeting just fell apart. His hyperbole was ridiculous. 'We've got a thousand projects. I can't finish anything without a new priority coming along.' Even his worst enemies were agreeing with him. What happened?"

"Uh. . . . I think they are looking for more focus," Gene said, trying to keep his voice flat, in a monotone.

"Of course, focus is their job. The committee is about strategic planning, isn't it? They are the ones who have been giving us focus. They are the ones who came up with the focus on undergraduate education, the focus on world-class-quality classroom experiences, and the focus on the adult learner."

Gene grimaced, "Not to mention the priority on equity in the workplace, the priority on fund-raising, the visibility of writing across the curriculum, the focus on science and computing literacy, the concern for civility, the student life improvement project, the campus-wide revisioning of the library and media resources, the budget equilibrium project, Reaching Out through Distance Education, the Center for Community Studies, the Year of Health, and the History Project."

"Are you saying that those aren't important? Are you saying that these things have not contributed to the university?"

"Well, no . . ." Gene said softly, "but let me ask you a question."

"You ask a lot of questions."

"What do you want to be known for after you leave the presidency?"

"Progress and change. Stupid question," she shot back.

Gene had taken a while to learn that Dr. Suarez loved heated exchanges and that he was always forgiven in the end. "And not scatter, confusion, and waste of resources." He tried, rather unsuccessfully, to look sly and clever as he said this.

"No! Where are you going with this?"

Gene hesitated, "I think that most of these projects are great, but I think what you are hearing, from me and the committee, is that they need to be tied together under the umbrella of a limited number of 'big ideas' on what is really, really important. Can you tell me what three things are most important to this university if it is to really say that it is achieving its mission and moving with strength toward its vision?"

"Why three? Why not two or five?"

"We can answer that question later. Right now, let's try for three."

"Well, I know that we have to provide the best possible education to our students to become successful members of society . . . so that they can think, compute, read, write and be good citizens . . . so that they can be productive members of society and contribute to the general commonweal . . . be ethical and aware of the environment. I know that the legislature wants to cut our funding and the federal government wants to control our prices. I know that our students are finding more difficulty feeling prepared for the changes in the job market. I know that companies are complaining about the 'quality' of all graduates, not just ours. I'm sorry Gene, I'm not in the mood to play games."

"No, no, let me try to extract the big things from what you've said. Here are three things: learning, affordability, and responsiveness. You said, 'provide the best possible education.' That is, of course, what we are all about—learning. Many of our priorities are admissions that we could do better, that we could understand this process better, that we could describe our successes better, that we could measure student learning better."

"I'm also picking up on your points about state and federal concerns and about what we have learned about our significant and ongoing market advantage—price. While efficiency may be an ugly word in academe, affordability is not. We must continue to invest in methods to bring efficiency to the process of producing learning. This means our administrative process especially."

"Finally, you emphasized the ever-changing world around us: employer needs, student needs, environmental needs, ethical challenges, technology developments. You know that we are more a battleship than a speedboat. Our success depends on our ability to be responsive."

The president studied Gene's face for a moment, "You know, however, that we could shoehorn all those projects and priorities under your neat three-pointed umbrella, but that wouldn't give us any more focus than we have now."

A slight, wry smile moved over Gene's eyes and mouth, "Yup," he said, "absolutely, but can you name the three most important things that we have to do to achieve affordability?"

"Oh I get it, like, uhh . . . , 1. persuade the legislature of the link between their funding and tuition. And, let's see, 2. the administrative 'best practices' project, and, uhm . . . how about, of course, 3. the 'no finance barriers' scholarship reform and fund-raising project?"

"I think we have something going here," Gene pronounced, arching his eyebrows.

"I suppose you've got this all worked out?"

"Let me look in the briefcase. I think I *did* put something together, but, of course, it's just something for you to build on."

"Of course," she mocked. "Then what?"

"You and I have to go out and say, 'Look we think these things are important. Here's why. If we can make progress here, then we can get to here.' I mean to the 'vision thing.' People will have other ideas. Many of them will be good. We'll keep changing and rewording, but we must not let it bloat."

"OK, OK. Let me see what you've got."

Gene reached into his briefcase for the sheet he had pulled off of his desk. "Here are some ideas," he said.

As he handed the sheet to her, she said, "Oh by the way, would you like some coffee?"

He could only grin. The meeting was over.

Seven Key Thoughts

1. Having a strategic attitude means having the right focus. Leaders are able to say, "This is important, today and tomorrow." They avoid saying, "Today's hot priority is . . ." Shifting attentions too quickly makes all attention shallow. This is not strategic. This is "day trading" for universities.

2. Leadership means being able to say, over and over, our mission is to serve these populations in these ways. Leaders need to be identified with the mission.

3. Leadership means being able to help people see the vision. "In five years I see a university that . . ." Leaders need to become identified with the vision as well. They need to lead others to "see" the vision.

4. Leadership requires the eloquent support and unceasing exploration of institutional values. Leaders must be able to proclaim what ways of doing things make the institution unique and respectable. People work for universities for respect as much as they do for money.

5. Leadership demands the continual invention of creative strategies for moving the organization toward the vision. The role of leaders vis-à-vis strategies is more like a godfather than an owner. Others put flesh on strategic bones. The leader picks the best of the lot.

6. Leadership requires the flexibility of expression of strategies to allow fast approaches to opportunities and lightning avoidance of blocks. Leaders point out the direction of the future, not the mechanisms. Under their protection, the best mechanisms grow and pull the university into the future.

7. Leaders celebrate the path. Celebrations are needed to give significance to the daily toil of each person in the university. Meaning is not easy to find in the modern world. People are grateful for the times that give them a small piece of meaning.

Chapter Thirteen

FINDING OPPORTUNITY THROUGH INSTITUTIONAL LEARNING

University administrators have a responsibility to institutionalize learning; figure 4 in chapter 2 shows the cycles that bring our focus back to beliefs, values, and vision. Lost learning is the worst manifestation of waste an organization can exhibit. Our unwillingness to share knowledge freely is one of the major causes of institutional forgetfulness. Without learning, the strategic organization drifts quickly back into the day-to-day organization.

When something is done once, it is an event. When the event becomes institutionalized, it is learned. Loss of strategic focus occurs because people forget what is important. Institutionalization can be as simple as keeping the president's cabinet agenda always organized along the lines of strategic directions. It can be as difficult as producing a budget document that demonstrates how the budget is accountable to the strategies.

All phases of strategic thinking require learning. Brochures and Web pages are opportunities for institutionalization. Learning also requires reflection. In reflection we ask, "What do we know now that we didn't know yesterday?"

There can be no taboo subjects for learning. We can learn about processes, and we can learn about our mission. We can learn new values and change our vision. Both our projects and principles are open to review. We can learn about our environment, including our competitors, and we can learn about ourselves—our strengths, and our shortcomings.

When a person learns, a fact, an idea, or a connection is remembered. When a university learns, the memory that is changed is embedded in the ritual of daily work. All members of the organization own the rituals. Evidence of learning comes when the new ritual is performed, as expected, by members. The daily rituals of the university are performed when we respond to e-mails, alter a Web page, or set a meeting agenda.

The following are some of the new rituals that need to be fostered to keep strategic thinking alive.

Auditing the mission. Is there a forum for criticizing the mission? Why is it now considered a blasphemous sacrilege to criticize the mission? Perhaps the mission is too narrowly stated. Perhaps it is far too broad. Have we identified those we intend to serve? Have we confined ourselves too narrowly to a limited methodology for reaching those we intend to serve? Has something changed in the world around us, or in our own capabilities and enthusiasms that recommends a new look at the mission?

Even if we only reaffirm the existing mission periodically, we will have learned in the process. We will know better who we are not. We will know that our mission is not to poorly serve some new group.

Auditing our principles. Principles are so complex they can seldom remain for more than a few semesters before they begin to decay. Over time our strategies get more grounded. Our vision gets clearer, and our values get more precise. This effort to see more clearly almost always has implications for principles as stated. Periodically, principles can be revised, cut, or added to.

Of course, people must be taught to expect regular revision. If not prepared, the campus community will be surprised and disappointed by a restatement. Revisions of holy works are not viewed with calm from all quarters. The sanctity can only be violated when there is already an expectation that organizational learning will lead to revision and that such learning is valued highly by the university.

Project evaluation. As discussed, project review is a necessary part of strategic thinking. (Dolence, Rowley, and Lujan [1997, 14] call project review "strategic learning.") What were the goals of this software implementation? Did we meet them? Did meeting them (or perhaps not meeting them) provide a strategic success—did we move toward our vision? Did we carry out the project within our values? If not, do we still believe in those values? Have we evolved any new rituals?

If we value our people, why did we lay off those Cobol programmers? Do we value people less than we thought, or did we fail to live up to our values? To learn, we must answer these questions. If we failed, how might we institutionalize a review of our values before we make the next critical decisions?

Learning about the university. Most strategic planning exercises call for an early expedition into the institution's "strengths and weaknesses." My impression of these exercises is that the strengths are fine celebrations of excellent characteristics, but the weakness lists are often just preliminary revelations of the coming list of plan projects. Lists of strengths and weaknesses require a strategic direction to deserve that name. A weakness that is unimportant in the strategic scheme of things is irrelevant. A liberal arts college that does not envision becoming a national-caliber research university should not list as a weakness its negligible physics research program.

A research university that puts strategic importance on its research reputation but is lagging in physics has a strategic opportunity, not really a weakness. I am uncomfortable when the exercise of enumerating strengths and weaknesses devolves into name calling.

A search for the "immutable" characteristics of the institution, which can be leveraged into strengths, can be equally frustrating. Many institutions see great advantage in their urban locations. I remember receiving a recruiting tape from one such institution, with lovely views of the exciting city and nothing of the university. Of course, suburban institutions with lovely campuses extol the virtues of beauty and safety. Then there are universities with locations in both zones, capturing all the advantages. If we read the history of any university, we will realize that location is hardly immutable. This supposed inherent strength is really a determined strategic direction.

Consider a college with a beautiful suburban campus that serves first-generation college-going students facing financial and academic preparation blocks. A second campus opened in an industrial building in the fringes of an urban area was also inundated with students. The strategic advantage was not the beauty of the original location, but the methodologies it had developed for serving its market.

A strength is only a strength in terms of whom the university has chosen to serve. These strengths can then be leveraged into strategic advantage. If a university has no strengths and thus no strategic advantages for serving any of its identified service populations, then it needs to go back and reexamine its mission. If it has strengths that serve no purpose for its identified service population, then it may also wish to go back and examine its mission to see if a new population that would be assisted by the strength should be included. This, however, is not a decision to be taken lightly.

The learning cycle for the institution is thus mission (service populations), strengths (nearly immutable characteristics), strategic advantage, then mission again, and so on. The cycle through the three areas should provide a harmonious run. Strengths should provide strategic advantage for service populations. If not, either the strengths should be ignored or the mission should be questioned.

Environmental scanning. Although scanning is often a major activity of the early stages of a strategic planning project (Dolence, Rowley, and Lujan, 1997, 6–7), this book emphasizes incorporating it into the weekly activities of a broad base of people within the university. The key difference, however, is developing a ritual of recording and disseminating key facts. Besides making the scan a small part of everyone's week, learning must occur within the university.

Changing the welter of facts that make up competitive tuitions into something meaningful is the challenge. This year public universities in many states are significantly raising tuition. While this may be interesting for many public colleges, it is strategically critical if viewed in terms of estimated net tuition for students at various income levels. The gap between public and private net tuitions at many income levels has narrowed significantly. Demonstrating this graphically as a comparison between the net tuitions of several close competitors prompts the revelation (learning) that competition is changing, to rest more on institutional responsiveness and the quality of the transformation and much less on price.

Learning can occur because of an institutionalized responsibility to make sense of the data. Who is scanning prices and is there a vehicle for presenting findings? Can we make everyone an "honorary researcher?"

Opportunity finding. Some institutions are entrepreneurial and some are not. Some seem to have roving bands of faculty and staff members out to make deals with few institutional constraints. Other universities take two years to approve a new course. Some universities confine entrepreneurial efforts to a few areas, like continuing education and distance learning. Strategic thinking requires management of opportunities, whether a "deal-a-day" or "confinement."

Opportunity finding can be viewed as one of the aspects of organizational learning. Managing requires understanding and guiding the rituals. The rituals have practitioners, rewards, punishments, guidance, assistance, and common prayers.

The holy book of opportunity finding should be the institution's principles. These can give guidance on where to look for opportunities and where not to look. Opportunities exist where there is a group of people who could be served better. Truly "finding" the opportunity, however, means coming up with a way, within the principles, of achieving the better service.

Opportunities may be found with new locations, new programs, new courses, new certificates, new degrees, new instructional modalities, new prices, new incentives, new times, or any number of other "new things." In many cases, however, this is the easy part. The hard part is defining the principles in a way that focuses attention on the strategic direction of the institution and also forces the entrepreneurs to answer the prior question, "Whom does this new thing serve better?"

The process requires incentives to flow smoothly. Identifying an underserved population within the mission of the institution and designing a competitively effective way of serving it require a great deal of effort. Learning must occur in two stages, the first requirement is identifying the underserved population. Then comes the "technology"—the manner of serving this group better. Finally, the whole thing is tested against principles, especially the part that reads, "in a way that does not draw resources away from existing, successful programs."

The university thus learns new capabilities, but it can only do so within a framework of incentives, like paying faculty members for developing new curricula, and constraints, like principles that anoint certain directions for strategic development.

Problem finding. An organization run by the three figures with eyes, ears, and mouth covered is one that will ultimately fail. Organizations fail to see blocks to achieving their vision for several reasons. First, bad news may be taboo. The shrine of the happy face is sanctified more than the shrine of learning. Messengers of bad news are shot. (And how often does a CFO have good news?) Efforts are made to hide the problem or clean it up before someone finds out (often exacerbating the original shortcoming).

The department that does not award tenure to a failing teacher is punished by having the slot taken away. The market researcher who shows declining market share is told to alter his data set and to keep the findings to himself. The admissions director who finds that prospective students cannot afford the university is fired.

In other cases, bad news would be dealt with calmly, but it becomes invisible. People who are locked into particular ways of seeing the world, who have particular ways of solving problems, often fail to see problems outside of their experience. Learning is possible in these organizations if the leadership team is broadened to include people who see the world differently. I even advocate adding deputies whose sole function is to find, report, and explore problems, augmenting the work of the internal audit department, where it exists.

Researching learning. We spend less in terms of a percentage of net sales on R&D on research to improve our core practices than nearly any other growth industry. What if we, like the microchip industry, spent 5 percent of our billions in sales on research into learning? We are seeing small spurts of progress from the work of cognitive psychologists and from challenges to the effectiveness of distance learning. It is good to see someone asking the question, "Do students seem to learn more in situation A or B?"

We are facing a conflict among three forces: the pressure to administer learning more efficiently, the democracy of student course choice, and the requirements of academic freedom. The theoretical perspective says that we should be rewarded for improving the technology of learning. We would be more accountable to legislators and tuition payers, if we could demonstrate that we were continuously improving the amount students learned for each dollar spent in the endeavor.

However, most of our attempts to pack in more learning per dollar increase the pain of learning. Students react by choosing less-painful subjects, methodologies, and instructors. Pain has a price that students evaluate in terms of lost wages (I took a sick day to study) and lost social contacts (I studied instead of partied). The more democratic and market based we allow college-, curriculum- and course-choice to be, the more students seem to retreat from our attempts at increasing learning efficiency.

Compared with attempts to legislate student choice, our attempts at legislating faculty choice seem even cruder. Academic freedom protects faculty members from outside meddling in course content (Balderston, 1995, 97).

Universities thus see little reward for learning about learning. Any institution that breaks this stranglehold will leap ahead.

Policy learning. I fear that most of our policies are merely copied from other institutions. A university ought to base its policies on data from its own institution. This does not always seem to be the case. If we ask an institution what *its* price elasticity is, we will undoubtedly get a blank stare. If we ask an institution what effect its alcohol policies have had on student drinking, or what has been the effect on diversity of its affirmative action policies, we may get the same stare. Does the institution make any effort to learn the effects of its policies, or does it merely think they are good ideas and what everyone else does? Research and the scientific method are the hallmarks of modern higher education. I do not think these concepts are sufficiently applied to administrative policies. This inhibition extends from mundane hiring policies to critical strategic ideas. Every strategy, concept, and value is a hypothesis that, if properly stated, can be tested. Is this marketing strategy working? How can we test it to see?

Avoiding the effort to learn about our policies and strategies is to be antilearning in a learning environment.

A Day in the Life: Sareena Collins, Budget Director, Grover Community College

Although it was late on a Thursday afternoon in November, Sareena felt a little more upbeat than normal for the time of day, week, and season. That morning she had received an e-mail announcing that the November edition of the *Strategic Times* newsletter for the college was available on the Web. The director of planning, Millie St. Claire, had asked her to write an article for it, and she was eager to see it in print. After a day of pulling together a special finance report for the president, she finally had time to look at the newsletter.

"Come and take a look," she said to her assistant, Bill Marley. Bill was walking by and looked over her shoulder.

"Page one," he said. "Not bad."

She knew he was about to tease. He often took a moment to find just the right jab. She thought she could divert him with quick comment. "I think Millie will want to use your instructional cost/price analysis next month. It's exactly the sort of thing she looks for."

Although his mouth was open, he merely took a sip of coffee and said, "Yeah, maybe." He went back to his desk.

Sareena's article was on the allocation of the previous year's budget expenditures by strategic priority. She knew that many people had wanted to know whether the college was doing more than just "talking the talk." She had worked with Millie to build a spreadsheet-based crosswalk that had allowed her to reclassify about 60 percent of the expenditures from within the accounting system. With the help of a bright work-study student majoring in accounting, she had been able to manually code another 50 percent of the remaining invoices and payroll expenditures to strategic priorities. Nevertheless, 20 percent of all expenditures could not be classified under a strategic priority.

The article showed how much had been spent in the three priority areas and in each of the 12 subareas. She had also talked about how she had done the study, and had concluded that it would be easier next year.

Then she noticed an article by the directors of governmental affairs and student financial aid on recent changes in the regulatory environment. There had been many changes in veterans' benefits, and the impact on GCCC could be large. The college had begun working with the base in the county many years ago, and the success of its programs had allowed it to begin providing distance-education courses to those in and no longer in the military.

There was a report from the values task force in the newsletter as well. The task force had started with the mission statement, "Educational Service to Improve the Lives of the People of Grover County" and had begun to explore what made GCCC a special place to work. She wondered, however, how widely held was the belief that all the citizens of the county, and not just the college's faculty, staff, and students, were the college's concern. If that were really true, the day-care center would be larger, and she wouldn't just be on the waiting list. She did agree that the value on service to the community was well enforced with academic support of student volunteers and internship experiences. Students could gain academic credit for these experiences if they could develop a learning contract on the experience and then exceed their learning goals.

The newsletter also had a piece that gave instructions on how to join the discussion on the president's new draft on the college's mission and principles. Through the college's Web site, faculty, staff, students, community members, and alumni were invited to post reactions, ideas, and responses to the comments of others in a streaming dialogue. Millie was the editor, but the article said that the president and strategic planning steering committee members had agreed to keep the discussions going and to take all comments seriously and give their support or qualifications in the Web dialogue stream. The software for this enterprise was the same as that used in their distance education courses. Sareena thought, "Well, that gives the distance education faculty and students an advantage."

She then glanced through a "Now and Then" column describing changes in student outreach. "We've come a long way," she thought. When the college first opened, counselors just visited high schools and talked to the senior classes about the advantages of GCCC. They usually timed their visits late in the year, so that they could appeal most directly to students who really had not done much thinking about college.

Now, GCCC faculty members, students, and counselors begin working directly with high school freshmen, helping them throughout high school to find the best postsecondary experience for each of them. Sareena's younger brother had told her with some amazement that he and two friends had met with a GCCC faculty member, a GCCC student, and two representatives of two other colleges, and they had told him that with his interest in science and animals, he would probably really like a bunch of higher education institutions other than GCCC or the other two represented colleges. They also told him that the key for his future would be to get his math grades up. At first he couldn't believe that they would try to sell him on another college; then he realized that they had really opened his eyes. Now he comes home so excited about marine biology that she can't believe it. "He always hated going fishing with Dad," she thought.

It was getting late, but she noticed a column on "Our Marketplace," talking about corporate training programs and how the college had become more of a player in that market. They had gone from viewing themselves as competing with in-house corporate education to a training and education broker in any environment: on campus, in house, and online. The college had put together a small team of people to work directly with large and small corporations in the county on needs assessments and partnering.

The back page had a lesson on county funding. Julie in institutional research had developed charts showing college support from the county, compared against all other community colleges in the state. There were graphs showing total dollars, dollars per student, support per capita in the county, support per capita as a percentage of average income, and support per student as a percentage of average income. Julie had been careful to say she was trying to avoid making a political point. While total revenues and revenues per student put the college in the lower third, per capita measures were in the upper third. In other words, the county may be providing less support, but it put a higher priority on the community college than other counties did.

Just then Grace Panemica from accounting walked by, saying, "Bill tells me you're leaving to go work for the *Herald Times.*" Out of the corner of her eye she could see Bill duck down.

"Well, did you read it?" Sareena said.

"Sure," Grace replied, "but I liked the article on working with high school students best. I had forgotten how much our attitude has changed about going out and grabbing kids."

"Yeah, it really has," Sareena said, and remembered that her brother would be home from college on Friday.

Seven Key Thoughts

1. Learning is evidenced by a mission that adapts to the needs of the world around us. We exist to serve. Not-for-profit universities are public trusts and will cease to exist if they do not satisfy any needs of the surrounding world. Seeking to understand this relationship requires an institutionalized ritual of learning.

2. Learning is evidenced when we go back and look at our principles to find that new, clearer values would cause us to restate the principles. Principles are highly dependent on transient knowledge. Our ideas about strategies, values, and even our vision are subject to revision. As the building blocks of principles, principles must shift as well.

3. Institutional learning can be recognized when we itemize concepts that are newly and widely understood. Conceptual understanding is always fragmentary and hypothetical. New data and new demands force us to improve our understanding.

4. Institutional learning is valued when there is an organizational eagerness to find opportunities. The vitality of a learning organization is evidenced by the way it has institutionalized the pursuit of opportunities. This pursuit requires the guidance of principles.

5. Institutional learning is valued when there is little fear to point out blocks in the path toward the vision. Blocks that stand in the way of achieving our mission, or even our projects, must be named, understood, and tackled. To avoid these blocks is contrary to the ideals of a learning organization.

6. Institutional learning is valued when there is evident comfort with the vision of the organization in an ever-changing, yet interesting, environment. The speed of environmental change appears to be accelerating as the complexity of our society increases. A learning organization is in a continuous cycle of comparing its vision to the environment and making adjustments.

7. Institutional learning must be codified and celebrated, or it will die. Institutions that do not make learning a ritual will become paralyzed, using the solutions of the last decade to solve today's problems.

Chapter Fourteen
SEVEN KEY THOUGHTS TO MOVE YOUR INSTITUTION FORWARD

1. Stop planning as a side exercise by an exclusive group. Strategic planning projects are not succeeding in bringing an orientation toward the future into everyday management. Strategic thinking should not be a separate effort from daily managing, nor should it only occupy the minds of an exclusive group.

2. Put little pieces of planning in every day. Strategic thinking must be part of daily work life. Not all things strategic are contained in a typical day. They must be parceled among people, made into "bite-sized" pieces, and made a part of daily routine. The Web environment greatly increases the opportunity to work independently but together.

3. Understand your environment. Strategic thinking requires a strong conception of the university in an environmental milieu. While an important portion of an administrator's job is to buffer core processes from external vibrations, these actions become enigmatic to others in the organization without an understanding of the institution's place in the competitive sea.

4. Survival is not a strategy; it's a reaction. Strategic thinking goes past survival. Survival is defensive. Strategic thinking is offensive. The goal is to thrive, not just survive.

5. If your university is not changing, but the environment is, then you are moving, but against the environment and not under control. Thriving in a dynamic environment requires change. Strategic thinking is a discipline of change.

6. Individual learning is not the same as organizational learning. For the organization to learn something that a member just learned, the idea has to be spread, codified, sanctioned, memorialized, and celebrated. Strategic plans are static because they do not include an institutionalization of learning. Strategic thinking requires that organizational learning to be dynamic.

7. Celebrate the path. Success is not reaching the goal. Success is always moving toward a new goal.

BIBLIOGRAPHY

Anderson, Richard E. *Strategic Policy Changes at Private Colleges*. New York: Teachers College Press, 1977.

Balderston, Frederick E. *Managing Today's University*. San Francisco: Jossey-Bass Publishers, 1995.

———. "Organization, Funding, Incentives, and Initiatives for University Research: A University Management Perspective." In *The Economics of American Universities*, edited by Stephen A. Hoenack and Eileen L. Collins, 33–52. Albany, NY: State University of New York Press, 1990.

Bensimon, Estela Mara, and Anna Neumann. *Redesigning Collegiate Leadership*. Baltimore, MD: The Johns Hopkins University Press, 1993.

Berger, Peter L., and Thomas Luckmann. *The Social Construction of Reality*. Garden City, NY: Anchor Books, 1966.

Birnbaum, Robert. *How Colleges Work*. San Francisco: Jossey-Bass Publishers, 1988.

Bossidy, Larry, and Ram Charan. *Execution: The Discipline of Getting Things Done*. New York: Crown Business, 2002.

Chait, Richard. "The Role of the Board." In *Strategy and Finance in Higher Education*, edited by William F. Massy and Joel W. Meyerson, 23–35. Princeton, NJ: Peterson's Guides, 1992.

Cohen, Michael D., and James G. March. *Leadership and Ambiguity*. New York: McGraw-Hill Book Company, 1974.

Cope, Robert G. *Opportunity from Strength: Strategic Planning Clarified with Case Examples*. ASHE/ERIC Higher Education Report No. 8. Washington, DC: Association for the Study of Higher Education, 1987.

Cyert, Richard M., and James G. March. *A Behavioral Theory of the Firm*. Englewood Cliffs, NJ: Prentice-Hall, Inc., 1963.

Dickmeyer, Nathan. "Balancing Risks and Resources: Financial Strategies for Colleges and Universities." *Business Officer* 16, no. 4 (October 1982): 14–17.

_____. "Budgeting." In *College and University Business Administration*, Fifth edition, edited by Deirdre McDonald Greene, 239–80. Washington, DC: National Association of College and University Business Officers, 1992.

_____. "Financial Aid's Share of the Pie." *Business Officer* 26, no. 7 (January 1993): 26–31.

Dolence, Michael G., Daniel James Rowley, and Herman D. Lujan. *Working toward Strategic Change*. San Francisco: Jossey-Bass, 1997.

Drucker, Peter F. *The Essential Drucker*. New York: Harper Business, 2001.

Dunn, John A., Nathan Dickmeyer, Peter T. Ewell, Hans H. Jenny, Dennis P. Jones, Donald J. Reichard, and Sean C. Rush. "Decision Processes." In *College and University Business Administration*, Fifth edition, edited by Deirdre McDonald Greene, 23–91. Washington, DC: National Association of College and University Business Officers, 1992.

Eckel, Peter D., and Adrianna Kezar. *Taking the Reins*. Westport, CT: American Council on Education and Praeger Publishers, 2003.

Emery, James C. "Conclusions." In *Financial Planning Models: Concepts and Case Studies in Colleges and Universities*, edited by Joe B. Wyatt, James C. Emery, and Carolyn P. Landis, 231–33. Princeton, NJ: EDUCOM, 1979.

Finnerty, Michael. "The Role of the Chief Financial Officer." In *Strategy and Finance in Higher Education*, edited by William F. Massy and Joel W. Meyerson, 51–65. Princeton, NJ: Peterson's Guides, 1992.

Fisher, B. Aubrey. *Small Group Decision Making: Communication and the Group Process*. New York: McGraw-Hill Book Company, 1974.

Gadiesh, Orit, and James L. Gilbert. "Transforming Corner-office Strategy into Front-line Action." In *Harvard Business Review on Advances in Strategy*, 153–73. Boston: Harvard Business School Press, 2001.

Gardiner, John J. "Building Leadership Teams." In *Leaders for a New Era: Strategies for Higher Education*, edited by Madeleine F. Green, 137–53. Washington, DC: American Council on Education and Macmillian Publishing Company, 1988.

Green, Madeleine F. "Leaders and Their Development." In *Leaders for a New Era: Strategies for Higher Education*, edited by Madeleine F. Green, 13–29. Washington, DC: American Council on Education and Macmillian Publishing Company, 1988a.

____. "Toward a New Leadership Model." In *Leaders for a New Era: Strategies for Higher Education*, edited by Madeleine F. Green, 30–55. Washington, DC: American Council on Education and Macmillian Publishing Company, 1988b.

Hauptman, Arthur M. "Quality and Access in Higher Education: The Impossible Dream." In *American Higher Education: Purposes, Problems and Public Perceptions,* 115–40. Queenstown, MD: The Aspen Institute, 1992.

Hopkins, David S. P., and William F. Massy. *Planning Models for Colleges and Universities.* Stanford, CA: Stanford University Press, 1981.

Hornstein, Harvey A. *Managerial Courage.* New York: John Wiley & Sons, 1986.

Kaplan, Robert S., and David P. Norton. *The Strategy-focused Organization.* Boston: Harvard Business School Press, 2001.

Karol, Nathaniel H., and Sigmund G. Ginsburg. *Managing the Higher Education Enterprise.* New York: Ronald Press, 1980.

Keller, George. *Academic Strategy.* Baltimore: Johns Hopkins Press, 1983.

Keohane, Nannerl O. "The Role of the President." In *Strategy and Finance in Higher Education,* edited by William F. Massy and Joel W. Meyerson, 37–50. Princeton, NJ: Peterson's Guides, 1992.

Knerr, Anthony D. "Financing Higher Education in a Global Economy." In *Financing Higher Education in a Global Economy,* edited by Richard Anderson and Joel W. Meyerson, 135–43. New York: American Council on Education/ Macmillian Publishing Company, 1990.

Kouzes, James M., and Barry Z Posner. *Leadership: The Challenge.* San Francisco: Jossey-Bass Publishers, 2002.

Kuhn, Thomas S. *The Structure of Scientific Revolutions.* Chicago: The University of Chicago Press, 1962.

Lahey, John. "Good Business, Thriving University." *University Business* 6, no. 8 (September 2003): 7–8.

LeLoup, Lance T. "From Microbudgeting to Macrobudgeting: Evolution in Theory and Practice." In *New Directions in Budget History,* edited by Irene S. Rubin, 19–42. Albany: State University of New York Press, 1988.

Meisinger, Richard J. *College & University Budgeting,* Second edition. Washington, DC: NACUBO, 1994.

March, James G., and Herbert A. Simon. *Organizations*. New York: John Wiley & Sons, Inc., 1958.

Martorana, S. V., and Eileen Kuhns. *Managing Academic Change*. San Francisco: Jossey-Bass Publishers, 1975.

Massy, William F., and Joel W. Meyerson. "Introduction." In *Strategy and Finance in Higher Education*, edited by William F. Massy and Joel W. Meyerson, 13-21. Princeton, NJ: Peterson's Guides, 1992.

McPherson, Michael S., and Gordon C. Winston, "The Economics of Cost, Price, and Quality in U.S. Higher Education." In *American Higher Education: Purposes, Problems and Public Perceptions*, 65-114. Queenstown, MD: The Aspen Institute, 1992.

Meisinger, Richard J., and Leroy W. Dubeck. *College & University Budgeting*. Washington, DC: NACUBO, 1984.

Miller, James. *Game Theory at Work*. New York: McGraw-Hill, 2003.

Morgan, Anthony W. "Budgeting Approaches in the 1980s." In *Financing Postsecondary Education in the 1980s*, edited by Fred F. Harcleroad, 47-65. Tuscon, AZ: Center for the Study of Higher Education, 1979.

Musashi, Miyamoto, *A Book of Five Rings*. Woodstock, NY: The Overlook Press, 1974.

Pearson, Gordon. *Strategy in Action*. Harlow, UK: Financial Times Prentice Hall, 1999.

Pfeffer, Jeffrey. *Managing with Power*. Boston: HBS Press, 1992.

Porter, Michael E. *Capital Choices*. Washington, DC: Council on Competitiveness, 1992.

____. *Competitive Advantage: Creating and Sustaining Superior Performance*. New York: The Free Press, 1985.

____. "How Competitive Forces Shape Strategy." In *On Competition*, edited by Michael E. Porter, 21-38. Boston: A Harvard Business Review Book, 1996a.

____. "What Is Strategy?" In *On Competition*, edited by Michael E. Porter, 39-114. Boston: A Harvard Business Review Book, 1996b.

Rowley, Daniel James, and Herbert Sherman. *From Strategy to Change*. San Francisco: Jossey-Bass, 2001.

Schaffer, Susan M. "The Stanford Experience I: The Financial Process." In *Strategy and Finance in Higher Education*, edited by William F. Massy and Joel W. Meyerson, 79–86. Princeton, NJ: Peterson's Guides, 1992.

St. John, Edward P. Prices, *Productivity, and Investment: Assessing Financial Strategies in Higher Education*. ASHE-ERIC Higher Education Report No. 3. Washington, DC: The George Washington University, School of Education and Human Development, 1994.

Tracy, Brian. *Turbo Strategy*. New York: Amacom, 2003.

Travers Robert M. W. *Essentials of Learning*. New York: MacMillian Publishing Co., 1972.

Tuckman, Howard P., and Cyril F. Chang. "Participant Goals, Institutional Goals, and University Resource Allocation Decisions." In *The Economics of American Universities*, edited by Stephen A. Hoenack and Eileen L. Collins, 53–75. Albany, NY: State University of New York Press, 1990.

Waggaman, John S. *Strategies and Consequences: Managing the Costs in Higher Education*. ASHE-ERIC Higher Education Report No. 8. Washington, DC: The George Washington University, 1991.

Warner, Timothy R. "The Stanford Experience II: The Financial Process." In *Strategy and Finance in Higher Education*, edited by William F. Massy and Joel W. Meyerson, 87–100. Princeton, NJ: Peterson's Guides, 1992.

Whalen, Edward L. *Responsibility Center Budgeting*. Bloomington, IN: Indiana University Press, 1991.

White, Joseph. "What Budgeting Cannot Do." In *New Directions in Budget History*, edited by Irene S. Rubin, 165–202. Albany, NY: State University of New York Press, 1988.